Connectors Collection #4 $\frac{11}{12}$

By Mary Ellen Hopkins

DEDICATION

To Sara Marie and Thomas Owen Hopkins

—Love, Grandma Hopkins

Grahic design and layout by JoAnn Armke, Capstone Publication Services, Encinitas, California
Photography by Michael Negley, Los Angeles, California

Direct inquiries to:
ME Publications
PO Box 1288
Cardiff by the Sea, California 92007

800-527-2665

www.maryellenhopkins.com

Contents

Getting started

Quilt designs

Designer worksheets

Author
Mary Ellen Hopkins

Technical Editor
David Hopkins

Photography
Michael Negley

Graphic Design
JoAnn Armke

ME Publications
PO Box 1288
Cardiff by the Sea, CA 92077 USA

www.maryellenhopkins.com

800-527-2665: orders

760-431-8928: fax

©2000 by ME Publications

No part of this product may be reproduced in any form, unless otherwise stated, in which case reproduction is limited to the use of the purchaser. The written instructions, photographs, designs, projects, and patterns are intended for the personal, noncommercial use of the retail purchaser and are under federal copyright laws; they are not to be reproduced by andy electronic, mechanical, or other means, including informational storage or retrieval systems, for commercial use.

The information in this book is persented in good faith, but no warranty is given nor results guaranteed. Because ME Publications has no control over choice of materials or procedures, the company assumes no responsibility for the use of this information.

Printed in Korea
ISBN 0-929950-25-9
Library of Congress Cataloging-in-Publication Data
Hopkins, Mary Ellen, 2000
Connector's Collection / Mary Ellen Hopkins
p. cm.
1. Patchwork–Patterns. 2. Quilts–Patterns.
3. Quick-Piece Quilting–Patterns. 4. Maching sewing.
I. Title.

What you need to know

So here we are, Year 2000 and another "Connector" book. Well, I just love them, and they're so versatile and EASY. My buzz phrase for this year is "DON'T BE A QUILT SNOB." In other words, don't turn up your nose over simple work. If you know the tricks for doing kindergarten work, you can create wonderful and original quilts.

This is not meant to be a project book, but rather a concept book. I have given you the tools to work with: Kansas Dugout, Double Kansas Dugout and the Loose Goose. Mix these with four-patches, cut squares and rectangles, and it's magic. I'm hoping the quilts shown here will give you the courage to strike out on your own. You should make piles of these blocks with lots of different fabrics and start laying out designs; you'll find there are a lot more possibilities than I have laid out for you in this book.

I'm a strong believer in making quilts for people you Currently Know and Love (versus heirloom quilts for people you have no chance of ever knowing).

What you need to have

None of the projects in Connector's Collection require unique or hard-to-find materials, notions, or supplies. You will probably find much of what you need—with the exception of fabric and batting—already in your sewing room.

Rotary cutter and mat

Use a large rotary cutter to quickly cut the strips and pieces needed for all of the projects. A self-healing mat protects the cutter blade as well as the tabletop.

Cutting guides

You will definitely need a 6"x12" ruler, and I also recommend a 4"x4" and a 6"x6" ruler to measure fabric and to guide the rotary cutter. There are many excellent rulers available; however, my favorites are the rulers by Salem Rule™ and Fiskars®.

Sewing machine

You don't need a fancy-shmancy machine: just a reliable, straight-stitch machine in good working order. Adjust the stitch length so the stitches hold seams securely in place, but are also easy to remove when necessary. The optimum seam allowance is 1/4". However, your seam doesn't have to be exact if you follow my PPM, Personal Private Measurement, methods. The PPM method will ensure precision and consistency of measurement throughout your quilt.

Thread

Use a good-quality, all-purpose or 100 percent cotton. Cotton-wrapped polyester sewing threads work too. Do not use prewaxed hand quilting thread in your sewing machine.

Pins

Use glass- or plastic-headed pins nearby. Long pins are especially helpful for pinning multiple, thick layers.

Iron and ironing board

These are essential because you'll want to press frequently and carefully to ensure accurately stitched results. An experienced quilter may tell you that she spends more time pressing than sewing.

Felt-covered foamboard

One of the most important accessories you can own is a felt-covered foamboard. This is your designing board where you can lay your smaller blocks out before sewing them together so that you can experiment with different colors and combinations. A 4 ft. by 8 ft. felt-covered foamboard works great, but if space is a problem a 4 ft. by 4 ft. size will suffice. Foamboard is available at most art supply stores. Use glue or spray adhesive to attach the felt. I attach only the overlap felt to the backside of the foamboard; this helps avoid any unwanted, glued-down wrinkles on the front.

Fabric selection & design

The colors used in a quilt create a mood or a feeling. We perceive colors in many ways. Some colors are clear. That is, they are pures, with no black, white, or any other color added. Other colors are muted. They can be tints, shades, or tones of the pure colors. Pure colors are often described as bold, crisp, vivid, bright, or dramatic. Often, colors can be intensified by their placement. A pure color next to black or white becomes striking.

Muted colors include a lot of variations that can be confusing to match in quilts. Adding white to a pure color creates a pastel or a tint. Adding black to a pure color softens it to become a shade darker than the original color. If grey is added to a pure color, it becomes a tone of the original color. For example, "country" colors such as dusty blues, mauves, buttery yellows, and grey-greens are tones of the original color.

Sometimes the print interferes with the perception of color, as in the case of the busy print or a fabric that includes many different colors. Stripes and plaids need special consideration when planning a quilt.

Aged fabrics have a special charm. The tea-dyed look involves overdying fabrics with tan dye or tea to create an aged look. Overdying can also rescue busy fabrics that are otherwise too dominating to put in a quilt. Another way to create a subtle look is to simply turn the fabric over and use the back side.

Color choice is very personal and should be approached with as much self-awareness as possible when choosing fabrics for a quilt. Many quilters are already in tune with the colors that feel right to them. They know exactly what colors they like to wear. Their homes are probably decorated in those same colors.

Choose the colors that are best for you!

Helpful hints

- Choose a fabric with many different colors in the print. Use this fabric to begin your color selection. Don't be afraid to experiment. Often a small amount of an unusual fabric can make a wonderful difference in the final outcome of your quilt.

- For a contemporary look, begin with a colorful plaid. Select solid colors, using the plaid as the starting place. Remember, you can expand a color by selecting darker or lighter shades within the same color family. Notice the amount of each color in the plaid in relation to the surrounding colors.

- When a quilt "glows" or has a color gradation from light to dark, the luminous effect is achieved by blending fabrics. Begin the block by selecting one very dark and one very light fabric. Gradually add medium colors in subtle tonal changes. These fill-in colors hold things together and create interest.

- Keep the color selection very simple. Use only shades of one color such as light, medium and dark blues. This is called a monochromatic color scheme. Don't worry. The variety of prints within each color choice will keep things from being boring!

Designing with worksheets

This is not just a book of quilts, it is a book of quilt concepts. Make each of your quilts your own. When you look at the instructions for quilts in this book, you will see that the quilts have not been completely colored in on the grid. Space has been left for you to get out your colored pens and experiment with color and how placement of color and value can alter the look of a quilt.

Learn how to make the basic Kansas Dugout and Loose Goose units, and let your imagination soar. There are limitless possibilities for designing your own unique quilts using these two units, especially when they are combined with four-patch and nine-patch units. I think one of the most valuable components of this book is the gridded worksheets. Here's where you can play with color, combine patterns and see what develops. It's great fun.

Rotary Cutting

These are basic rotary cutting guidelines that will help you complete the projects in this book.

The pieced projects in Connectors Collection are created without templates. You'll cut all strips using a rotary cutter, then crosscut strips into smaller segments and combine them to complete the necessary blocks and units. ME NOTE: Reverse the following rotary-cutting techniques if you are left-handed.

1. Do not bother refolding factory fold to match selveges; it doesn't matter...trust me. Place the fabric on the cutting mat so that the length of fabric lies to your right, with the raw edges on the left. Fold by bringing the factory-folded edge to the top-most selvage, making the top and bottom folds parallel.

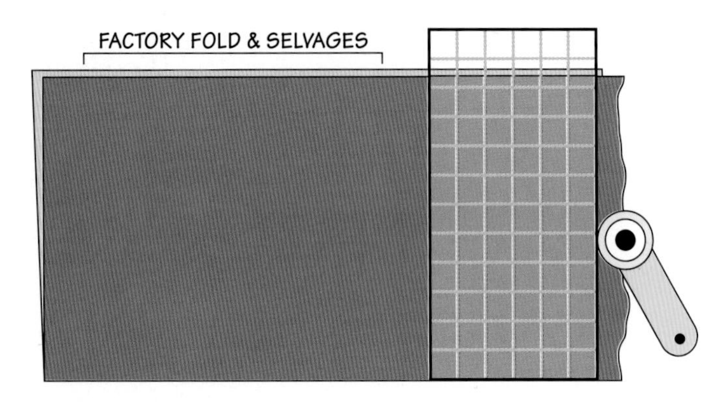

2. Align your 6 x 12 in. ruler with the fold, and press firmly on the ruler to keep it from moving. Place the cutter blade next to the ruler and, exerting an even pressure on the rotary cutter, begin cutting, trimming away the uneven edge.

   Always roll the cutter away from your body! As you cut, walk your fingers along the ruler to hold it steadily in place. Before you remove your ruler, make certain that all the layers have been cut. If not, repeat, and apply more pressure to the cutter.

3. Keeping the fabric to your right, use the ruler to measure a strip of the appropriate width from the left straight edge. If, for example, you need a 3 in. wide strip of fabric, align the fabric edge with the 3 in. line on the ruler and cut along the ruler's right edge.

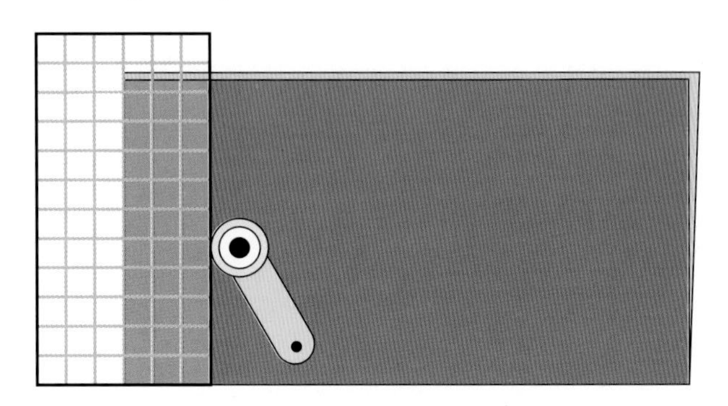

4. Turn the strip horizontally and cut to the desired shape and size. I recommend a 4 x 4 in. ruler for these cuts.

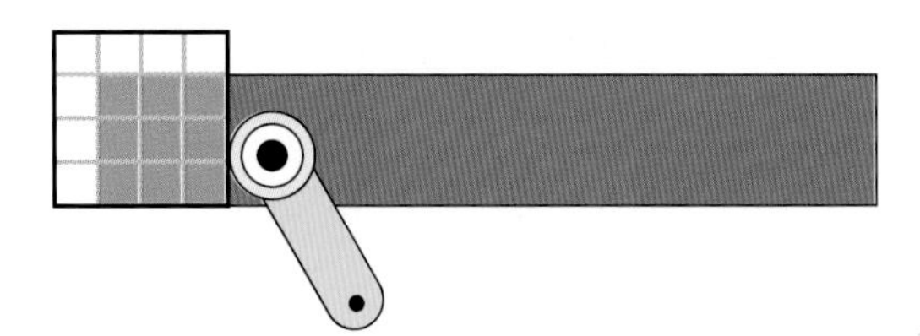

Pressing

Place a freshly laundered, folded towel on the ironing board when pressing blocks. The towel helps ease out any unwanted fullness, so the project will lie flat.

Do not use steam. It can distort pieces (especially smaller ones) and even alter the block shape. Use a spray bottle with water instead. As a rule of thumb, set your iron on the cotton setting, but always test the temperature when working with white-on-white fabrics because they tend to scorch.

Develop the habit of pressing each seam as it is sewn. Turn the piece over and "tack press" by lightly touching the iron to the seam allowance to get it started in the right direction. On the front side, spray lightly and press with gentle pressure from the center out. Check the back of the block to make sure all seams are pressed correctly before proceeding.

PPM: Personal Private Measurement

PPMs are created from the measurements you have chosen for your initial block and strip sizes. Your chosen measurements will remain the same throughout the project. Another very important and simplifying aspect to the PPM method is that you never need to make calculations or adjustments for seam allowances!

I will never instruct you to use a specific measurement. Instead, you will chose the starting sizes. Only you know if you are making a wall hanging or a king-size quilt, and only you know what particular look you are trying to achieve.

Basic Rules of PPMs

1. **Seam allowance**: the distance between the stitching and edge of the fabric. The measurement of the distance can be any size.

   It is only important that the seam allowances remain the same. Some people prefer an exact quarter inch. I use the inside edge of the presser foot and the edge of the fabric as a guide. I don't know exactly what size seam allowance that gives me…and I don't care! I will never calculate using that measurement or ever make any adjustment for it.

2. **PPM 1:** The width of the first and narrowest strips used in a project will be your PPM 1. For example, if the starting strip sizes are 2 in. wide, than PPM 1 equals 2 in.

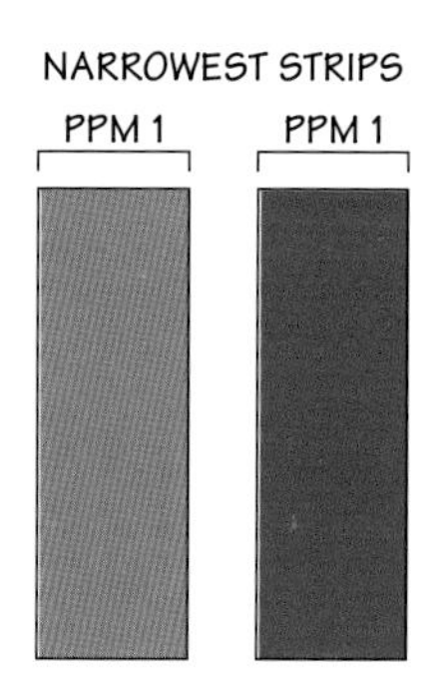

3. **PPM 2:** In many projects you will form wider strips by sewing two or more strips together. Lay two PPM 1 strips on top of each other with the right sides together. Sew strips together on one edge. After strips are sewn and pressed, use a ruler and measure the width. The width of the two sewn strips will be your PPM 2. Or, in the case of a nine-patch, your PPM 2 will be the measured width of three strips sewn together as shown on page 9.

   Remember that you must determine your PPM 2 by actually measuring it with your ruler. Do not calculate the width by subtracting seam allowances from seam widths. This method will insure much greater accuracy as your project grows…trust me.

NARROWEST STRIPS SEWN TOGETHER
PPM 2
PPM 1

ME NOTE: Sew all pieces along one edge (using your presser foot as a guide). Press open from the right side, pressing the seams in the same direction. (See instructions for pressing on page 9 and instructions for 2sey's, 4sey's and Beyond! on page 10.) This will help insure that the seam spreads fully and consistently.

In many projects, you will see arrows indicating in which direction to press seam allowances. When seam allowances meet, alternating the pressed direction of a seam allowance will avoid clumps of overlapping seams on the reverse side of your project. In addition, matching seams will butt together perfectly if seam allowances are pressed in the opposite directions. Do not press open the seam allowances unless specifically directed to do so. Open seam allowances don't work very well, and it takes a lot more time!

Four-patches & nine-patches

Matching points

When sewing the fabric pieces that make up a unit or a block, follow the individual piecing diagrams. Press each group of pieces before joining it to the next unit.

There are several techniques you can use to get your seams to match perfectly. I prefer the opposing seams method: when stitching one seamed unit to another, press seams in opposite directions. The opposing seams will hold each other in place and evenly distribute the fabric bulk. Plan pressing to take advantage of opposing seams. You will find this particularly important in strip piecing.

OPPOSING SEAM ALLOWANCES

ALIGN SEAMS AND RAW EDGES

ME NOTE: Please note that the Loose Goose unit (page 13) is an exception to the rule.

Strip piecing

Many of the quilts in this book contain simple units based on four-patch or nine-patch units. Strip piecing is a quick and easy way to mass produce these units. It eliminates the long and tedious repetition of sewing together individual pieces.

To make four-patch or nine-patch units, first cut strips across the crosswise grain of fabric as shown on page 6.

Four-patch units

1. Sew light and dark strips of your PPM 1-width fabric together to create one or more strip sets. Press seam allowances toward the darker fabric, pressing from the right side so the fabric won't pleat along the seam lines. Usually, pressing toward the dark fabric will result in opposing seams. The width of these sewn-together strips is your new PPM 2.

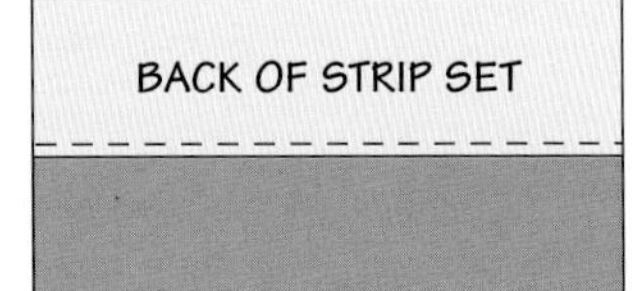

2. Layer two strip sets with right sides facing and with seams and colors in opposite directions.

PLACE RIGHT SIDES TOGETHER, NESTING SEAM ALLOWANCES

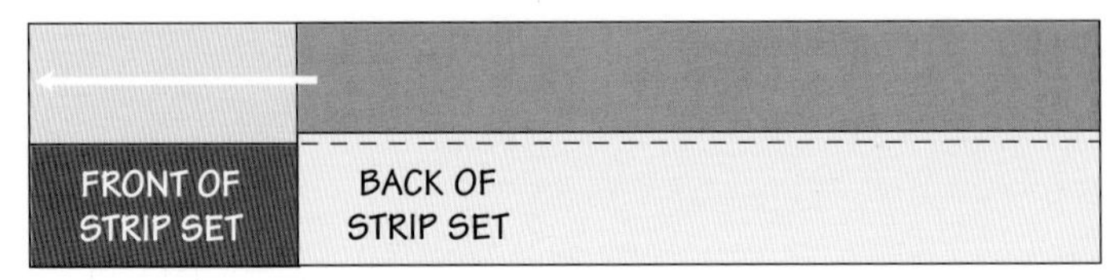

3. Using your ruler, cut the strip sets into pairs of PPM 1-wide segments, beginning at the left side and working toward the right. The width of the cut is specified in the directions for each quilt.

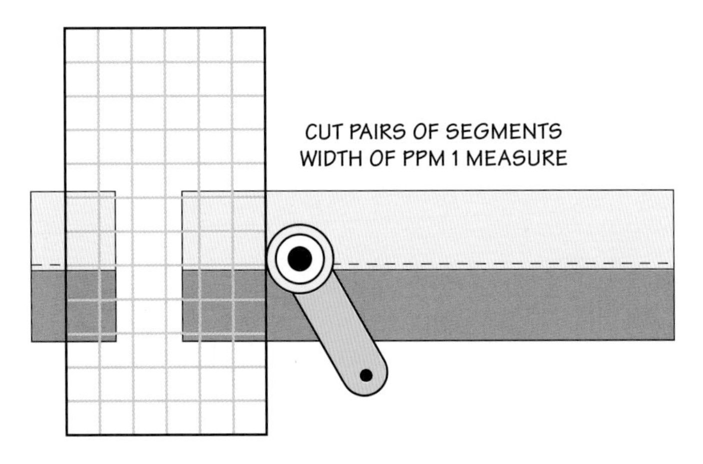

4. Stitch pairs together as illustrated to complete a four-patch unit.

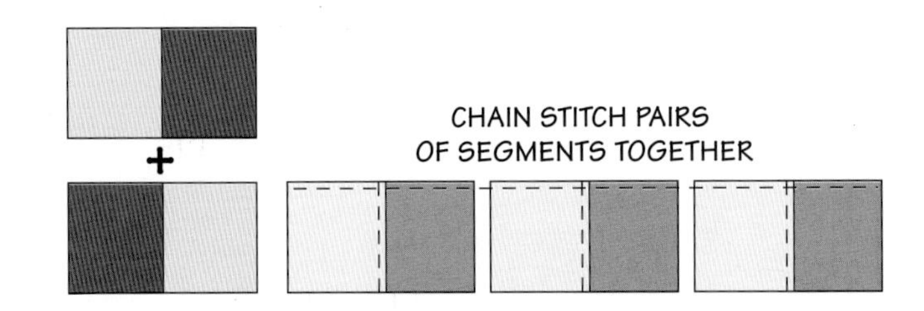

5. Press seam to one side.

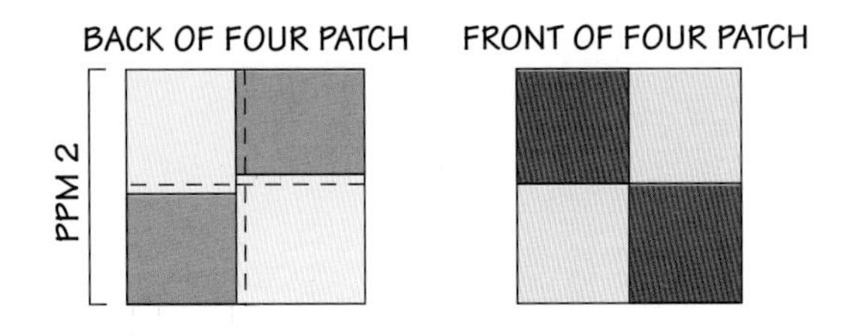

Nine-patch units

Nine patches are made using the same principle as four-patch units but with three strips of fabric. You need to make two different strip sets.

1. To make Strip Set 1, sew one light strip between two dark strips. The strip width is your selected PPM 1. Press seams toward the dark fabric.

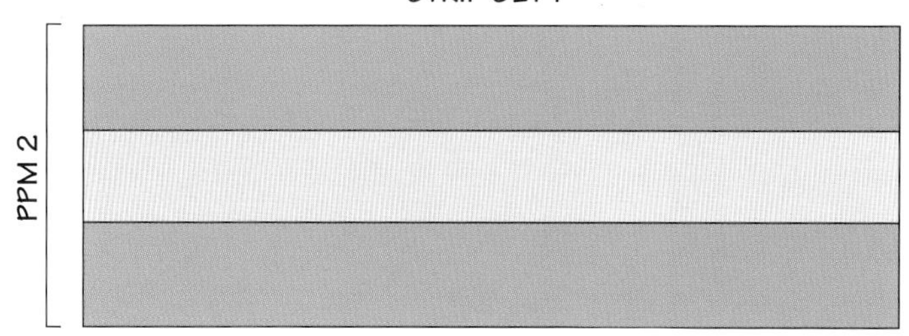

2. To make Strip Set 2, sew one dark strip between two light strips, using quarter-inch seams. Press seams toward the dark fabric.

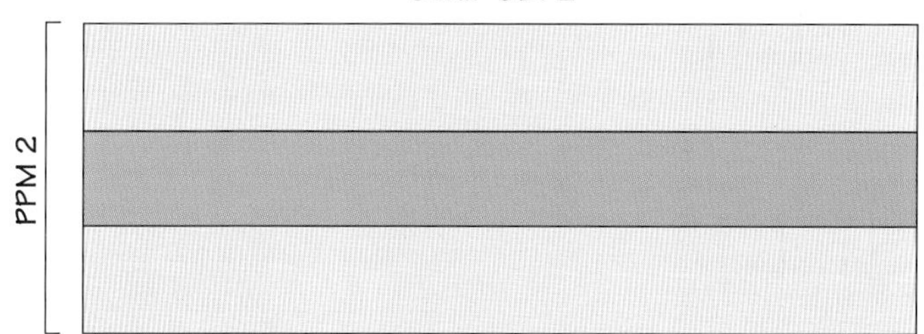

3. Place Strip Set 1 on Strip Set 2, with right sides facing. The seam allowances will be in opposing directions.

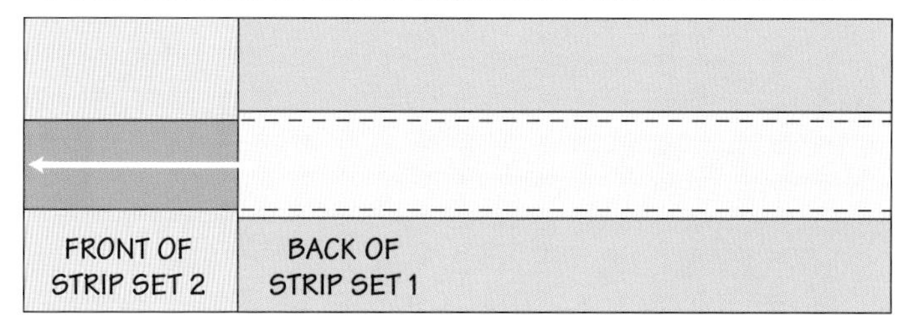

4. Cut strip sets in pairs. Begin at the left side of the strip and work toward the right. The width of the cut is specified in the directions for each quilt.

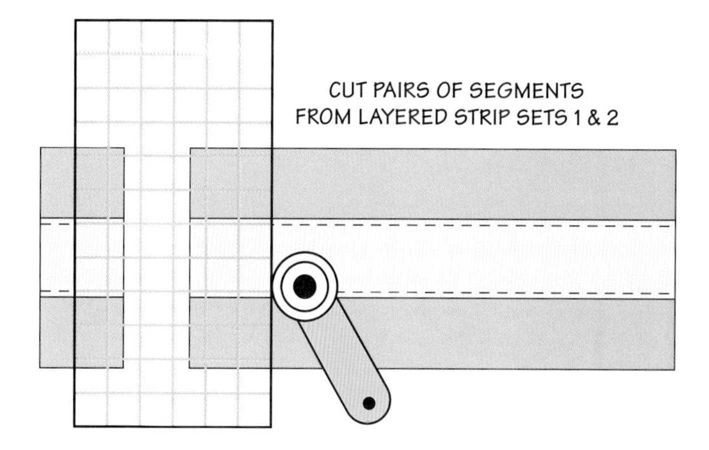

5. Stitch pairs together. These may be chain stitched.

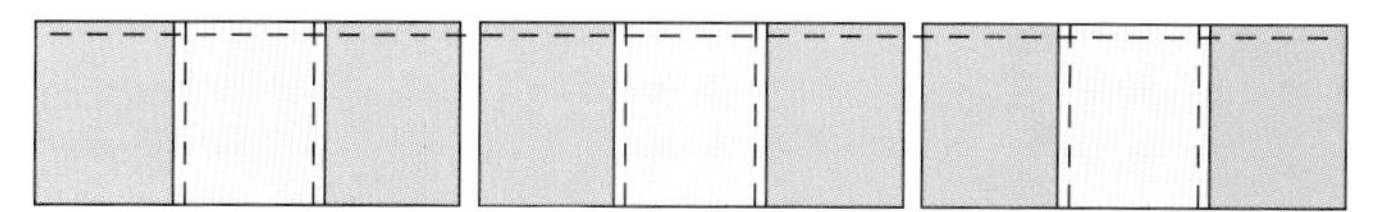

6. Cut the remaining Strip Set 1 into pieces the same width as the pieces you cut for the pairs in Step 4.

7. Chain stitch the remaining pieces to the previously sewn pairs to complete the units.

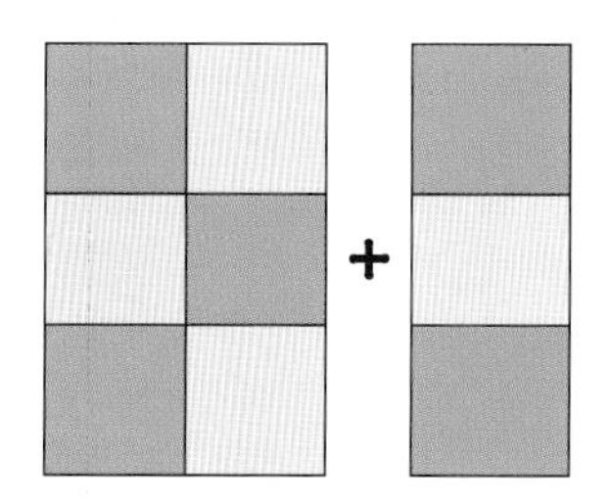

8. Press seams as shown below.

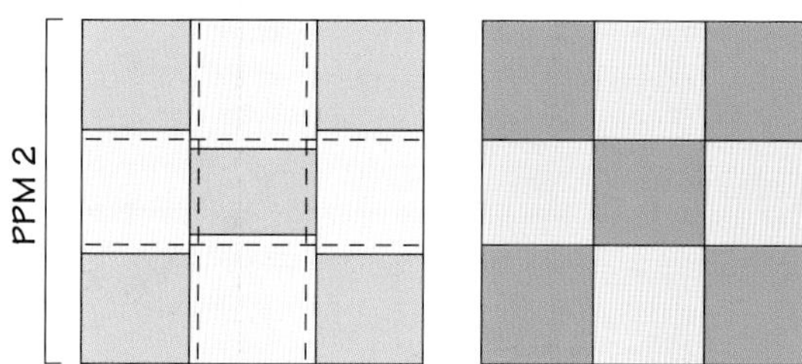

Kansas Dugout

We all know how easy the Kansas Dugout block is to make…and it has a diagonal shape! I've told you over and over, "the more simple the block, the longer the play-time." So, I once again prove my point…

Connectors

The connector method of sewing angles is accurate, less intimidating, and easier than using templates! When sewing angles, place the fabrics right sides together and draw a diagonal line on the wrong side of one of the pieces. Use a fine-point marker or sharp pencil to draw the line at the angle shown in the illustration. Sew exactly on the drawn line and cut away the excess fabric, leaving a quarter-inch seam allowance.

To sew a connector to a larger square:

1. You can draw diagonal line on the wrong side of the small square, but I skip this step by starting my needle in one corner and veering to the right in a slight curve to the opposite corner.

2. With right sides together, lay the connector square over the background square as shown in the illustration; make sure the diagonal line lies in the proper direction for your particular unit.

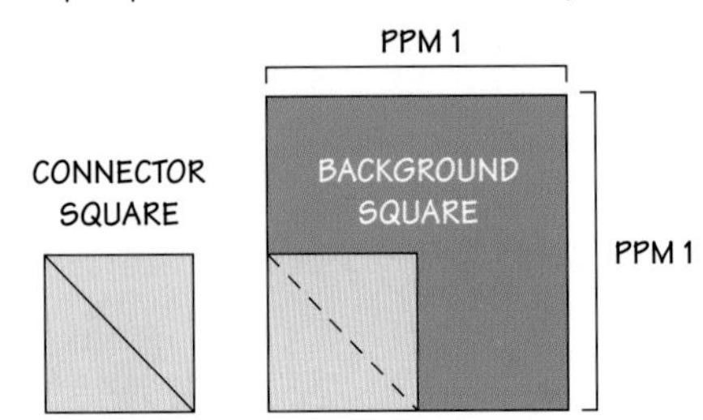

3. Stitch directly on the diagonal line and cut away the excess fabric, leaving a quarter-inch seam allowance.

ONLY TRIM CONNECTOR PIECE! DO NOT TRIM BACKGROUND FABRIC.

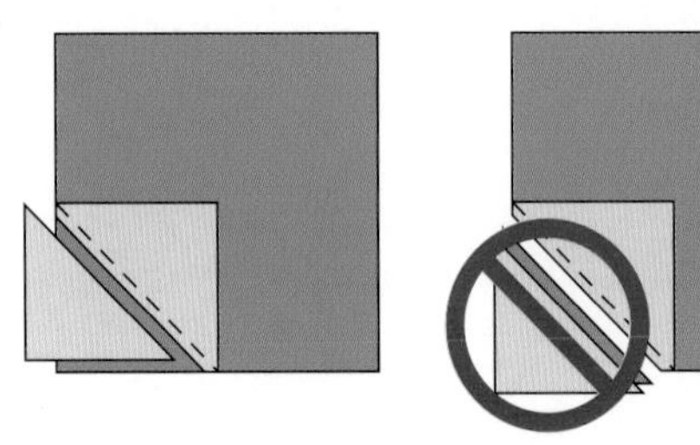

Do the same in the opposite corner. You must cut off the excess fabric BEFORE you press the connecters back to the corners so that you will know where to press to.

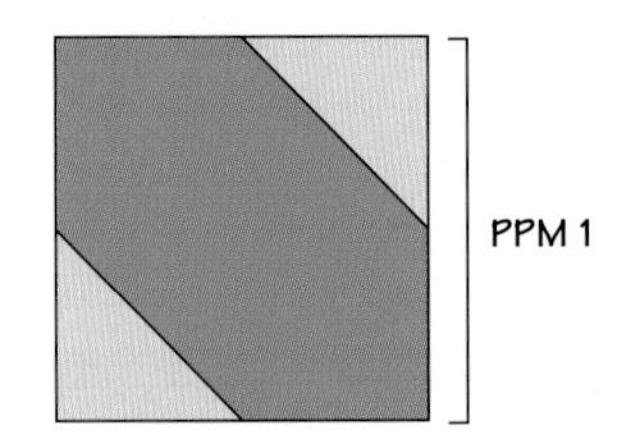

Double Kansas Dugout

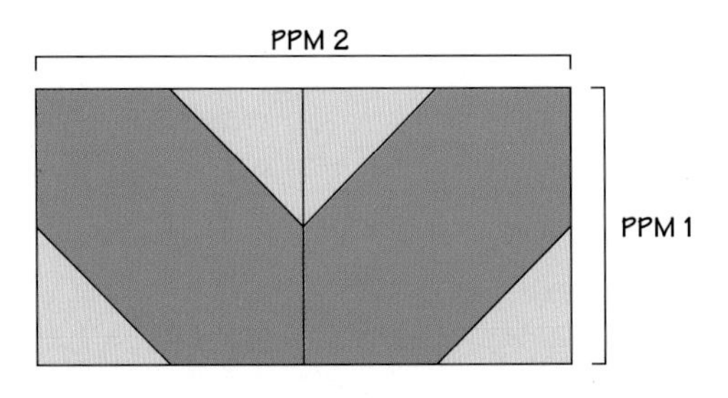

CUT BACKGROUND SQUARE	FINISHED SIZE	CUT CONNECTOR
2 1/2"	2"	1 1/2"
3"	2 1/2"	1 3/4"
3 1/2"	3"	2"
4"	3 1/2"	2 1/4"
4 1/2"	4"	2 1/2"
6 1/2"	6"	3 1/2"
8 1/2"	8"	4 1/2"

Loose Goose

The Loose Goose is a kindergarten unit that is sewn together with a single seam. Make one unit, and you'll understand why the goose is called "loose."

Loose Goose units often are combined in a design with Double Kansas Dugouts. Here's how to make a Loose Goose that will be the same size as your Double Kansas Dugouts.

1. Measure your PPM 1 (Kansas Dugout) and cut 2 background squares using that measurement.

CUT 2 BACKGROUND SQUARES PPM 1 MEASURE

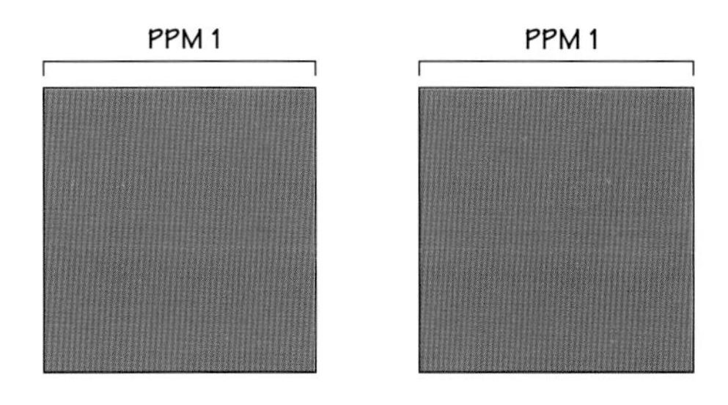

2. For your "goose" cut a rectangle that is PPM 1 wide and the length of two PPM 1's minus one-half inch.

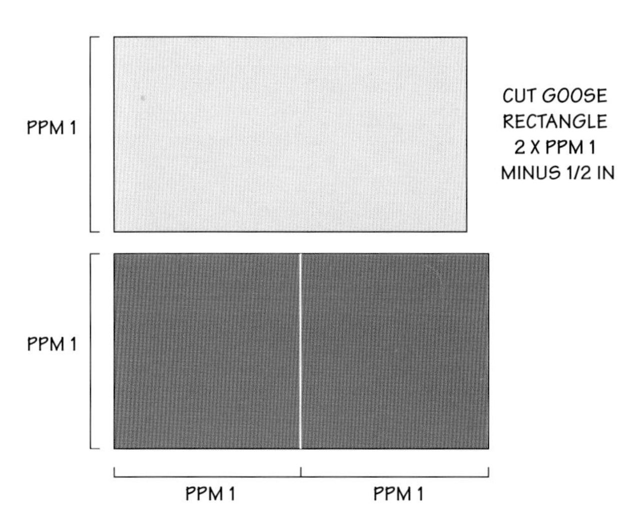

3. Fold the goose rectangle in half with right sides on the outside.

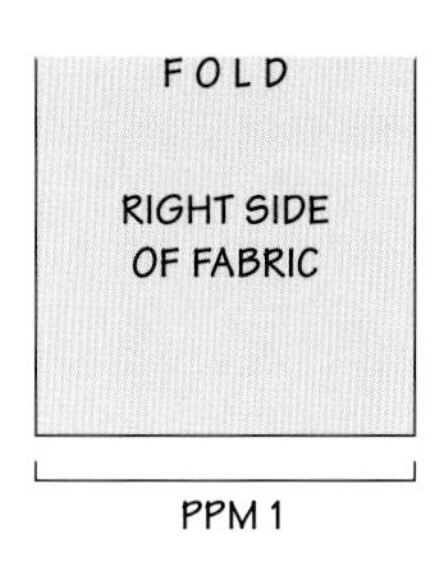

4. Place the two background squares together, sandwiching the folded goose rectangle in between, all raw edges together. Stitch across the fold of the goose.

SANDWICH THE FOLDED GOOSE PIECE BETWEEN THE RIGHT SIDES OF BACKGROUND SQUARES; ALIGN THE BOTTOM EDGES AND BOTTOM CORNERS OF ALL 3 PIECES. STITCH ACROSS THE FOLD OF THE GOOSE.

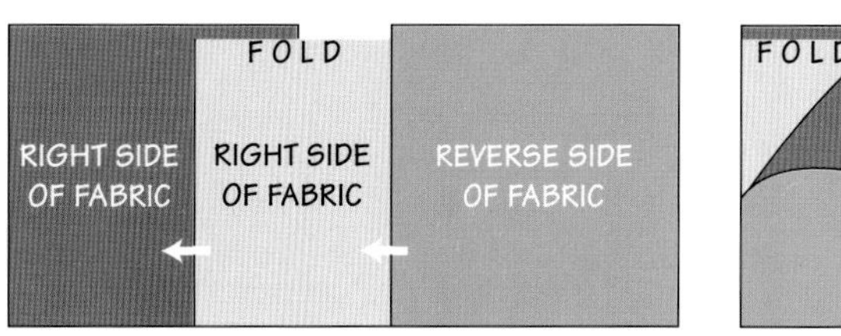

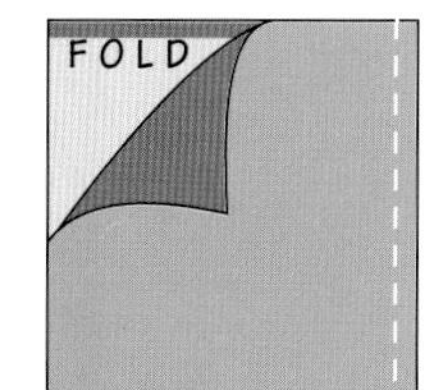

5. Open the background pieces. To shape the goose, align the fold of the goose piece on top of the seam, align raw edges at the bottom, flatten the goose and press. ME NOTE: Press the seam open! Do not press the seam to one side because it creates too much bulk with this piecing method. This goose is loose; you do not need to stitch the sides of the goose.

OPEN PIECES AND FLATTEN.
FOLD OF GOOSE WILL ALIGN WITH SEAM.

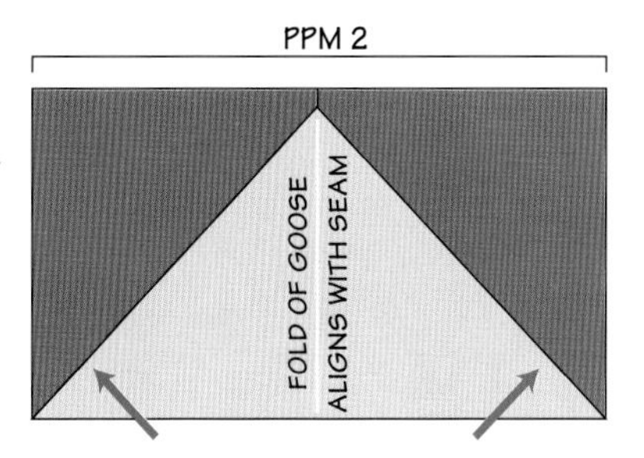

THIS "GOOSE" IS LOOSE

IF BACKGROUND SQUARES ARE CUT	THEN CUT GOOSE PIECE
2 1/2"	4 1/2"
3"	5 1/2"
3 1/2"	6 1/2"
4"	7 1/2"
4 1/2"	8 1/2"
6 1/2"	12 1/2"
8 1/2"	16 1/2"

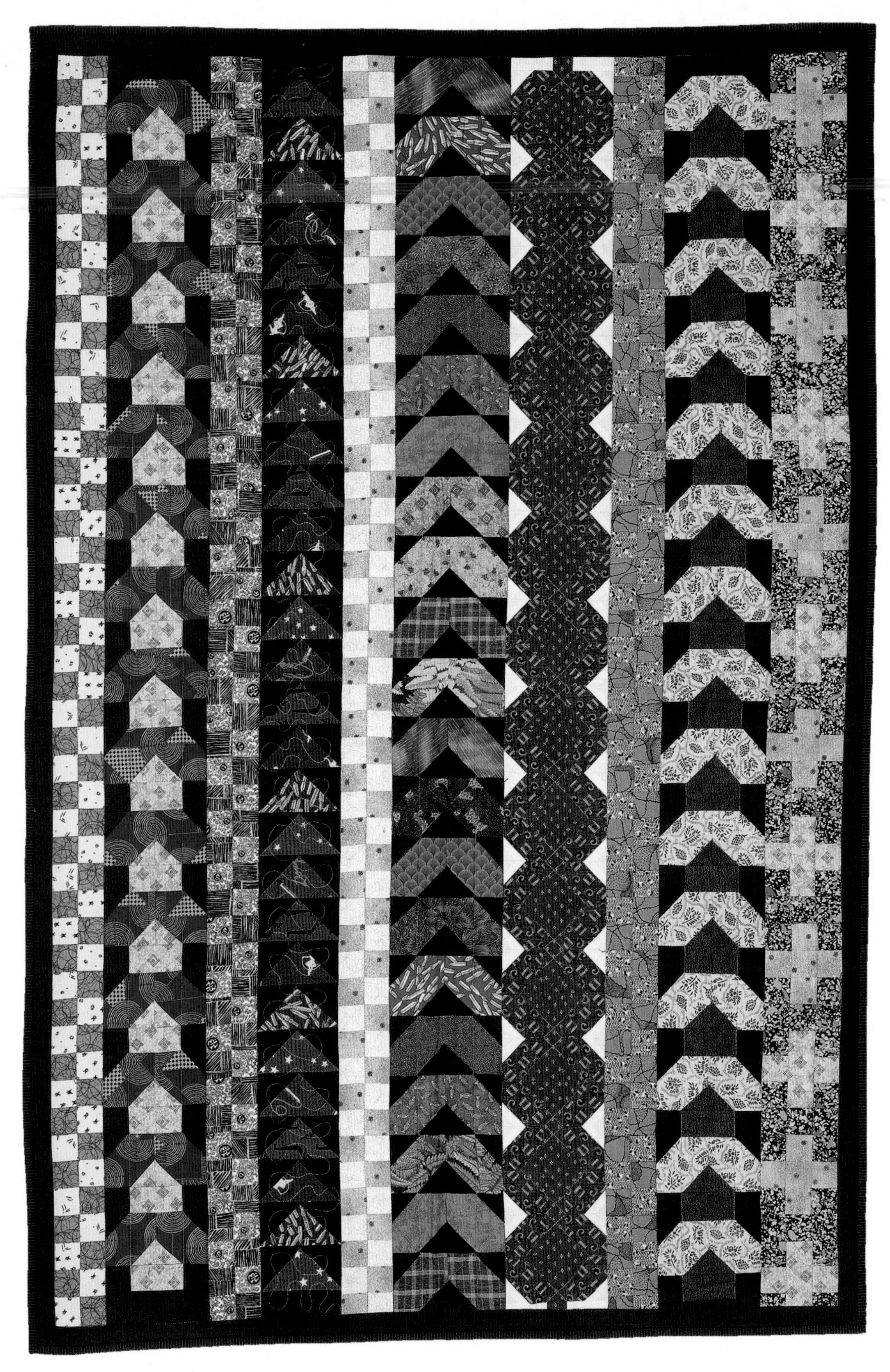

Strippy Quilt

Pieced by Mary Ellen Hopkins, Pacific Palisades, Cal.

Strippy Quilt

This quilt is pieced from long vertical "strips" made from three (more if you want) different blocks: four-patch, Loose Goose, and double Kansas Dugout. If you want your rows to line up, make the four-patch first, and the measured dimensions of that completed four-patch will be the PPM 1 for your Loose Goose and Kansas Dugout background units. HOWEVER, as you can tell by the photo, MY rows of strips do not line up at all. I just used pieces on the floor left over from other quilts. Looks fine to me. This was just meant to be a "davenport" quilt. The illustation shows only one option; you can put the strips in any order you want.

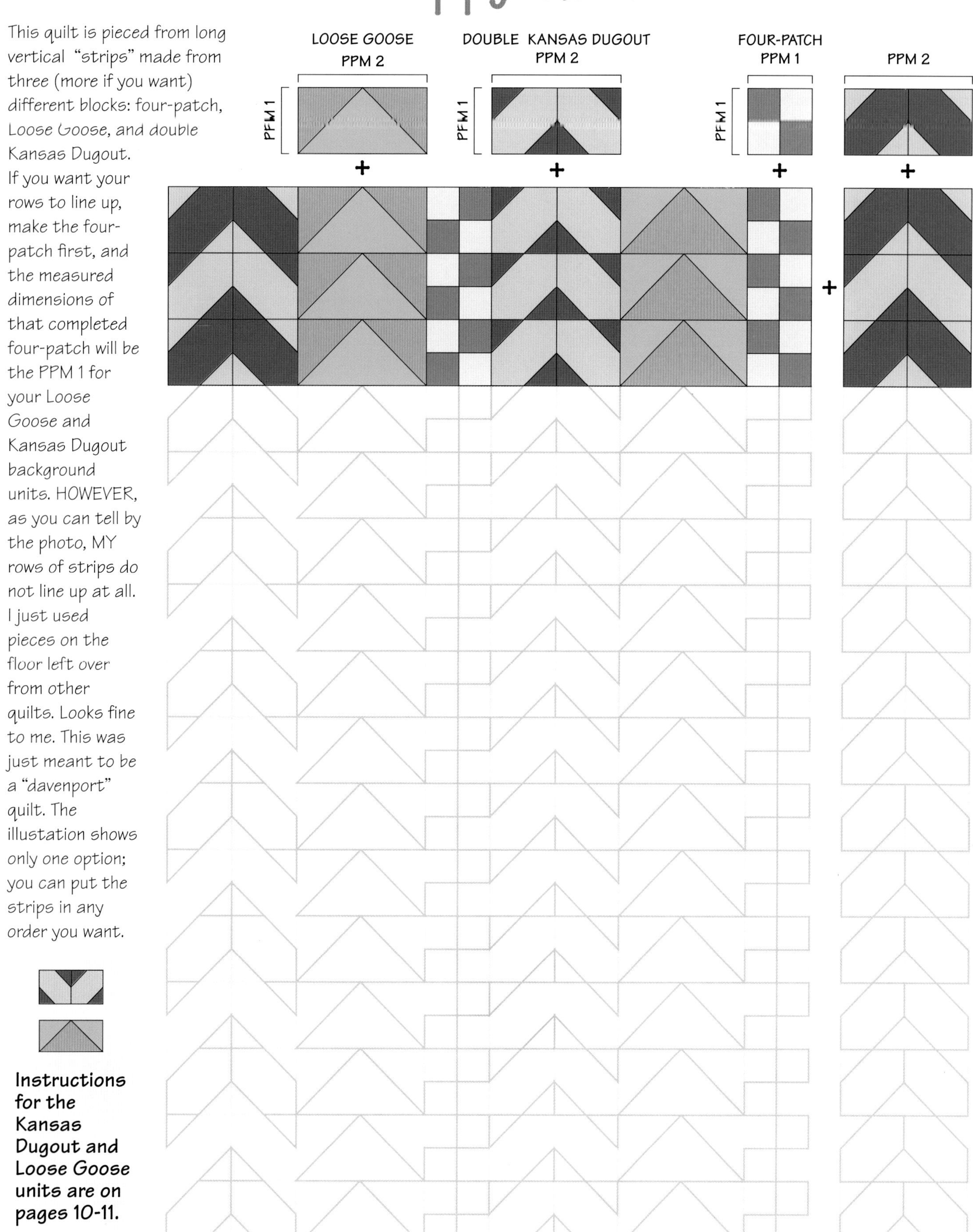

Instructions for the Kansas Dugout and Loose Goose units are on pages 10-11.

You may photocopy this page for your personal use to experiment with coloring your design; this page is not for distribution.

Pieced by Mary Ellen Hopkins,
Pacific Palisades, Cal.

Poor Man's Tibetan Fishnet

Pieced by Teri Antholz,
Quintessential Quilts,
Reedsburg, Wis.

Poor Man's Tibetan Fishnet

This design is made from two simple units, the Kansas Dugout and strip-cut rectangles. Half of the Kansas Dugouts have light backgrounds, and half have dark backgrounds. The quilt is set together in horizontal rows—Kansas Dugout rows are set alternately with rows of pieced rectangles.

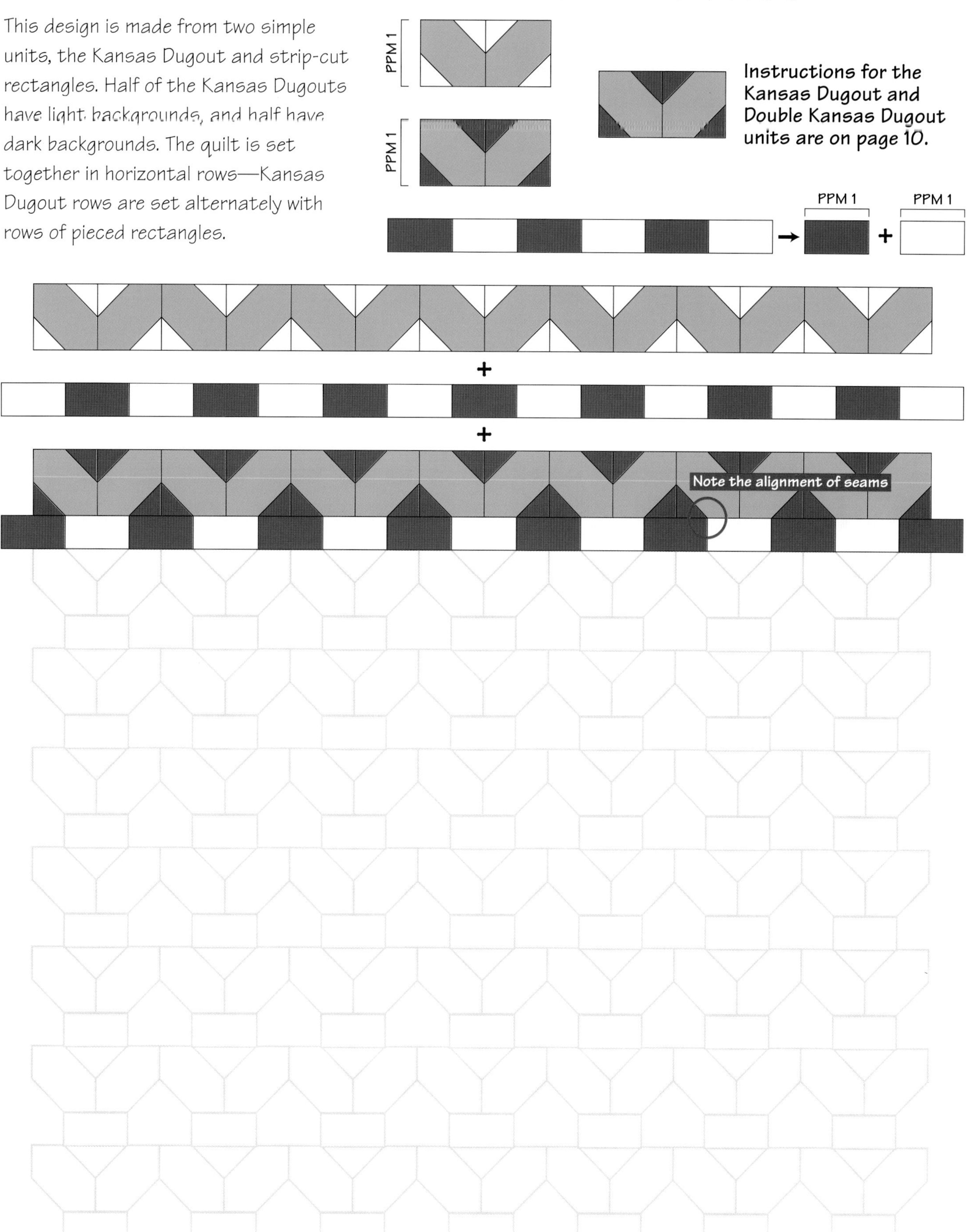

You may photocopy this page for your personal use to experiment with coloring your design; this page is not for distribution.

Poor Man's Tibetan Fishnet Variation

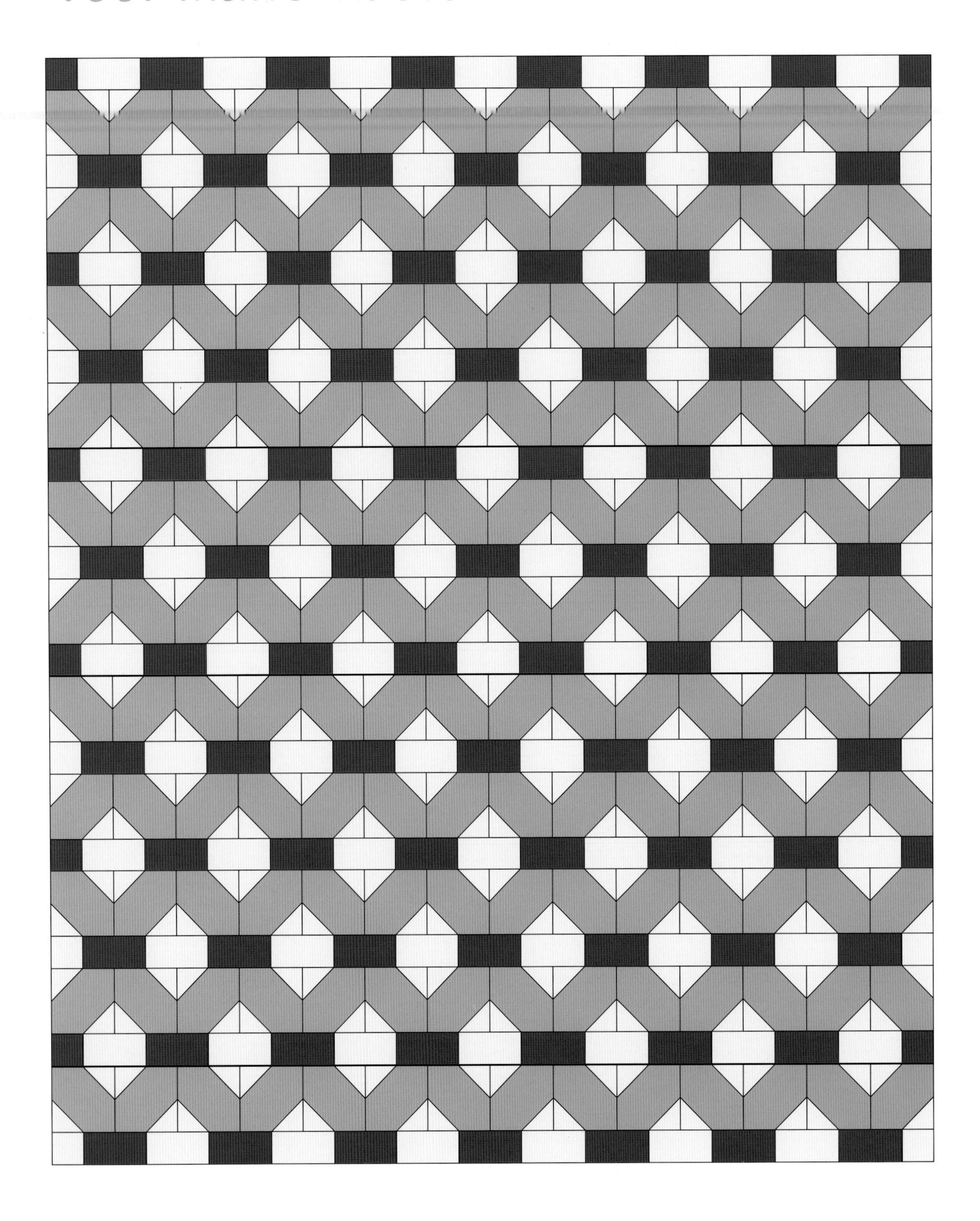

Poor Man's Tibetan Fishnet Variation

Once again, this design variation is made from two simple units, the Kansas Dugout and strip-cut rectangles, sewn into rows the width of the quilt.

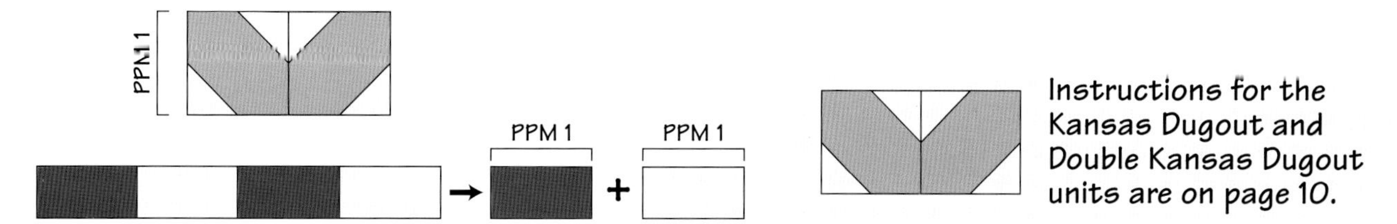

Instructions for the Kansas Dugout and Double Kansas Dugout units are on page 10.

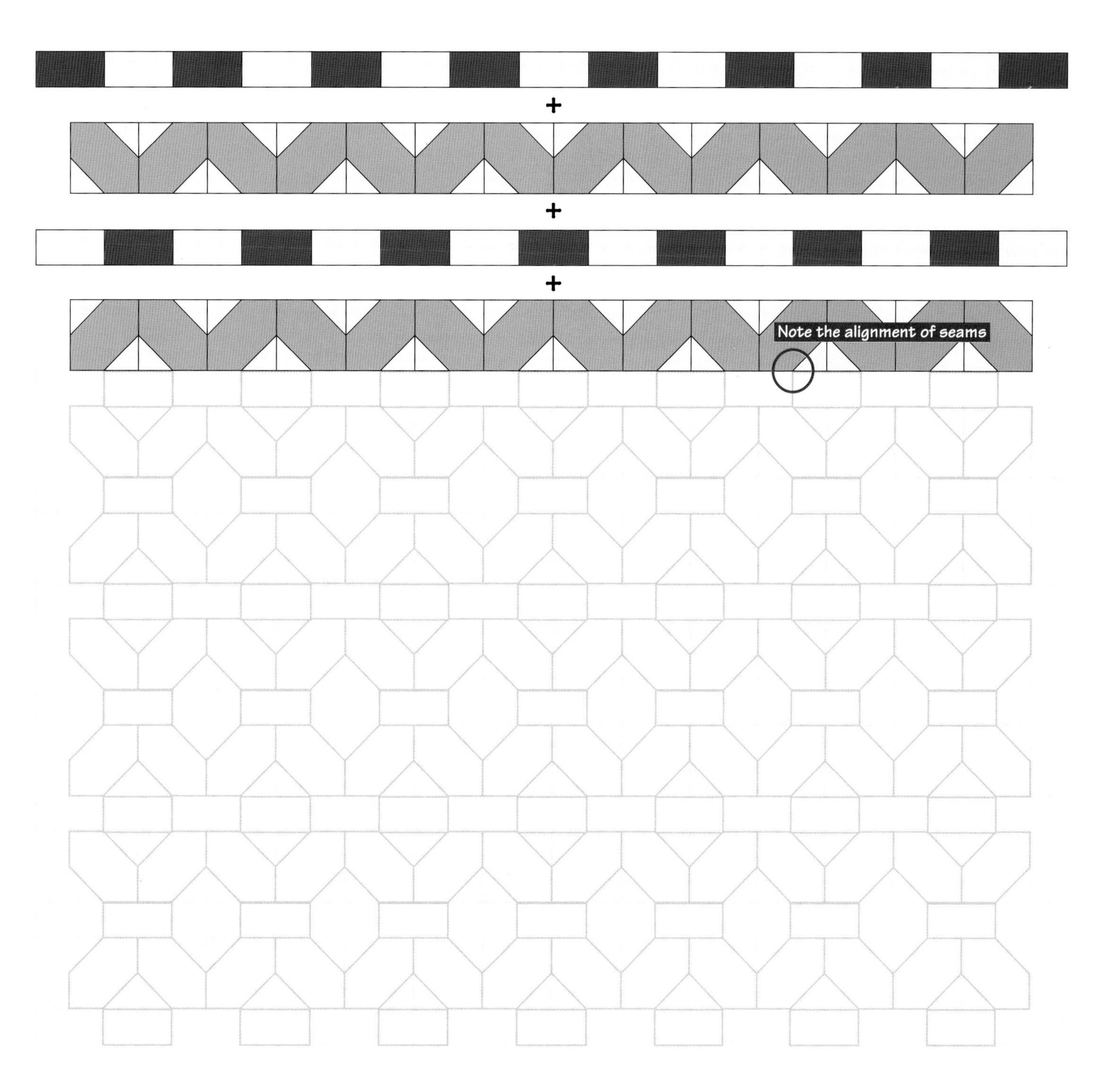

You may photocopy this page for your personal use to experiment with coloring your design; this page is not for distribution.

Pieced by Lisa Sasaki,
Los Angeles, Cal.

A Magnificent Mesh!

Pieced by Mischelle Hart,
The Quilted Sampler,
Tampa, Fla.

A Magnificent Mesh!

This design is made from three simple units, the Loose Goose, the Kansas Dugout and strip-cut rectangles. You will need equal numbers of Loose Goose and Kansas Dugout units. The cut length of rectangle strips is the PPM 1 measure; the width is whatever pleases your eye. The quilt is set together in horizontal rows.

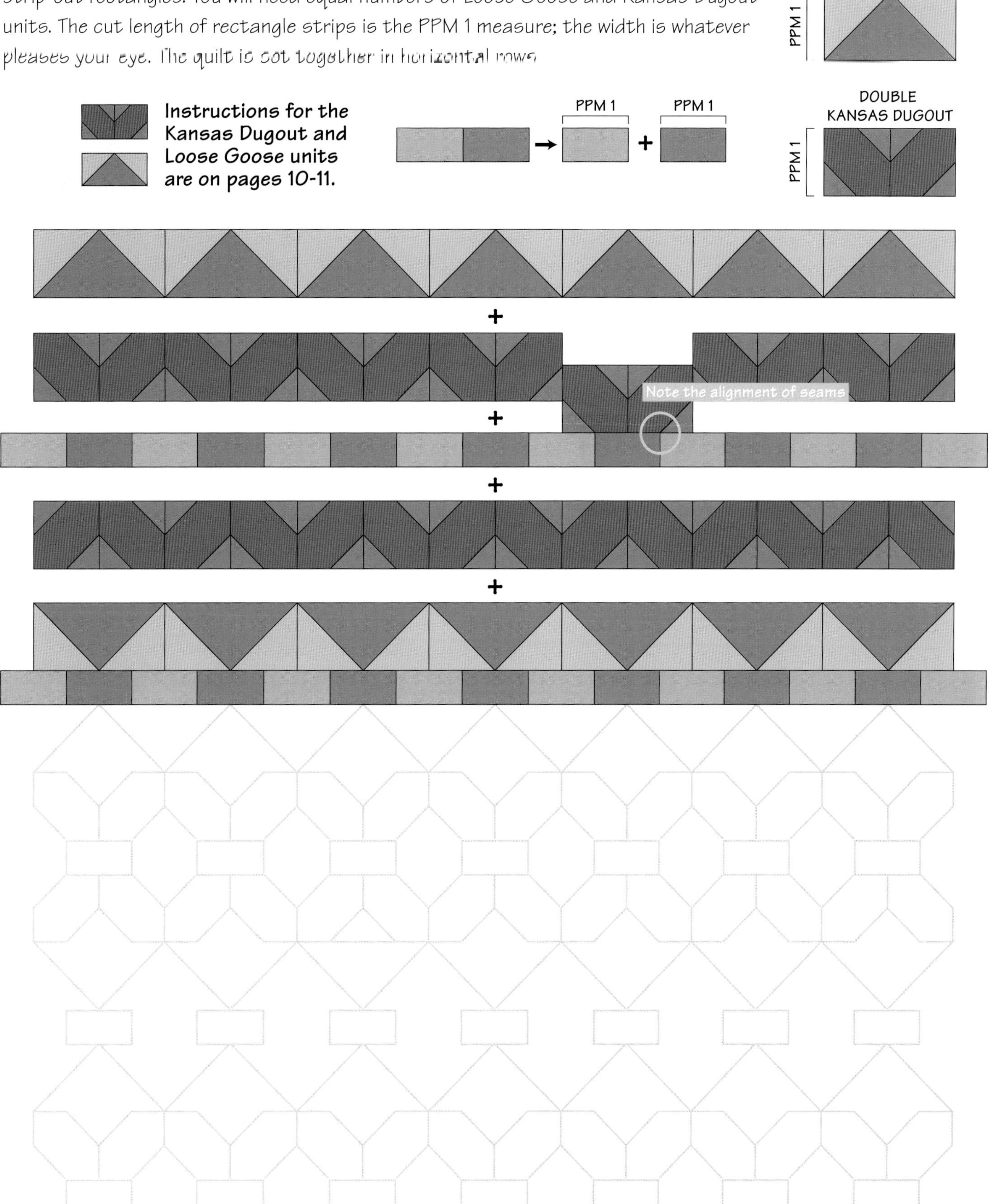

You may photocopy this page for your personal use to experiment with coloring your design; this page is not for distribution.

Tapestry

Both quilts pieced by Mischelle Hart,
The Quilted Sampler,
Tampa, Fla.

Mischelle Hart has given us an extraordinary example of a TINY baby step—she simply replaced the black fabric in the quilt at left with a light fabric in the above quilt. All other fabrics stayed in the same position. What a difference.

Pieced by Marilyn Nelson,
R. Lily Stem Quilts,
Modesto, Cal.

Pieced by Mary Beth Haus,
Oklahoma City, Ok.

Tapestry

Pieced by Mary Ellen Hopkins,
Pacific Palisades, Cal.

Pieced by Katrin Lehmann,
Rastede, Germany

This quilt actually is the variation shown on page 50, It Was a Very Long Flight

Tapestry

Kindergarten blocks make a Tapestry. All you need are equal amounts of Double Kansas Dugout and Loose Goose units. After you have colored in the design, just lay a ruler across each horizontal row to see what colors you need to piece. You can control your horizontal zig zags best by piecing in horizontal rows.

You may photocopy this page for your personal use to experiment with coloring your design; this page is not for distribution.

Tapestry Variation

Pieced by Nancy Podolsky, Modesto, Cal.

Tapestry Variation

This design is created from Loose Goose, modified Loose Goose (see Pinwheels, p. 38), pieced and plain strips and modified Kansas Dugouts.

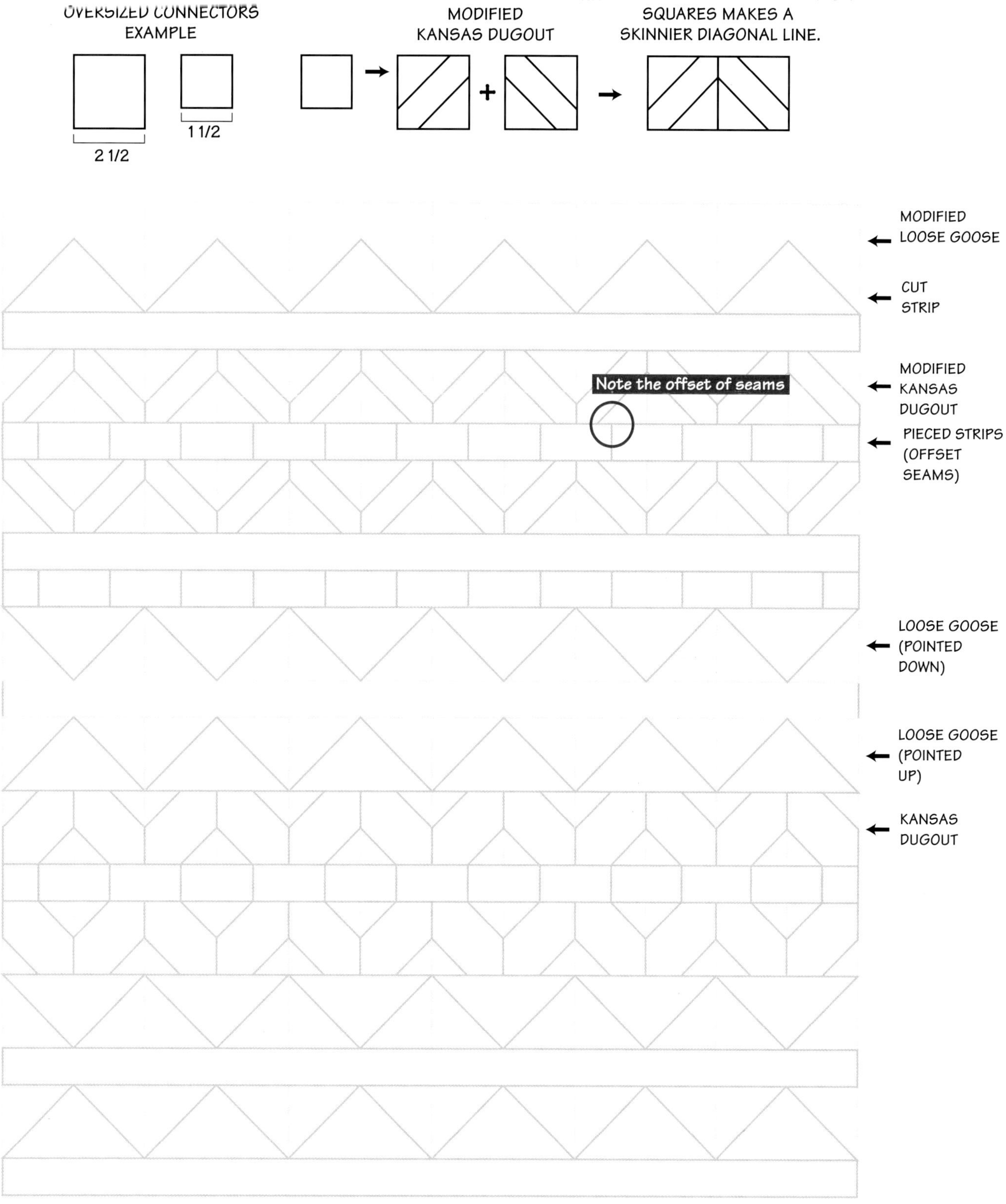

THIS CONTINUES ON DOWN AS SEEN IN QUILT

You may photocopy this page for your personal use to experiment with coloring your design; this page is not for distribution.

Double Spools

Pieced by Diana Marshall,
Oatley Cottage, Australia

Double Spools

This intricate design uses only two simple blocks—the Loose Goose and the Kansas Dugout. It's the way you use your fabric that takes a little thinking. Laying your blocks out before sewing really helps here.

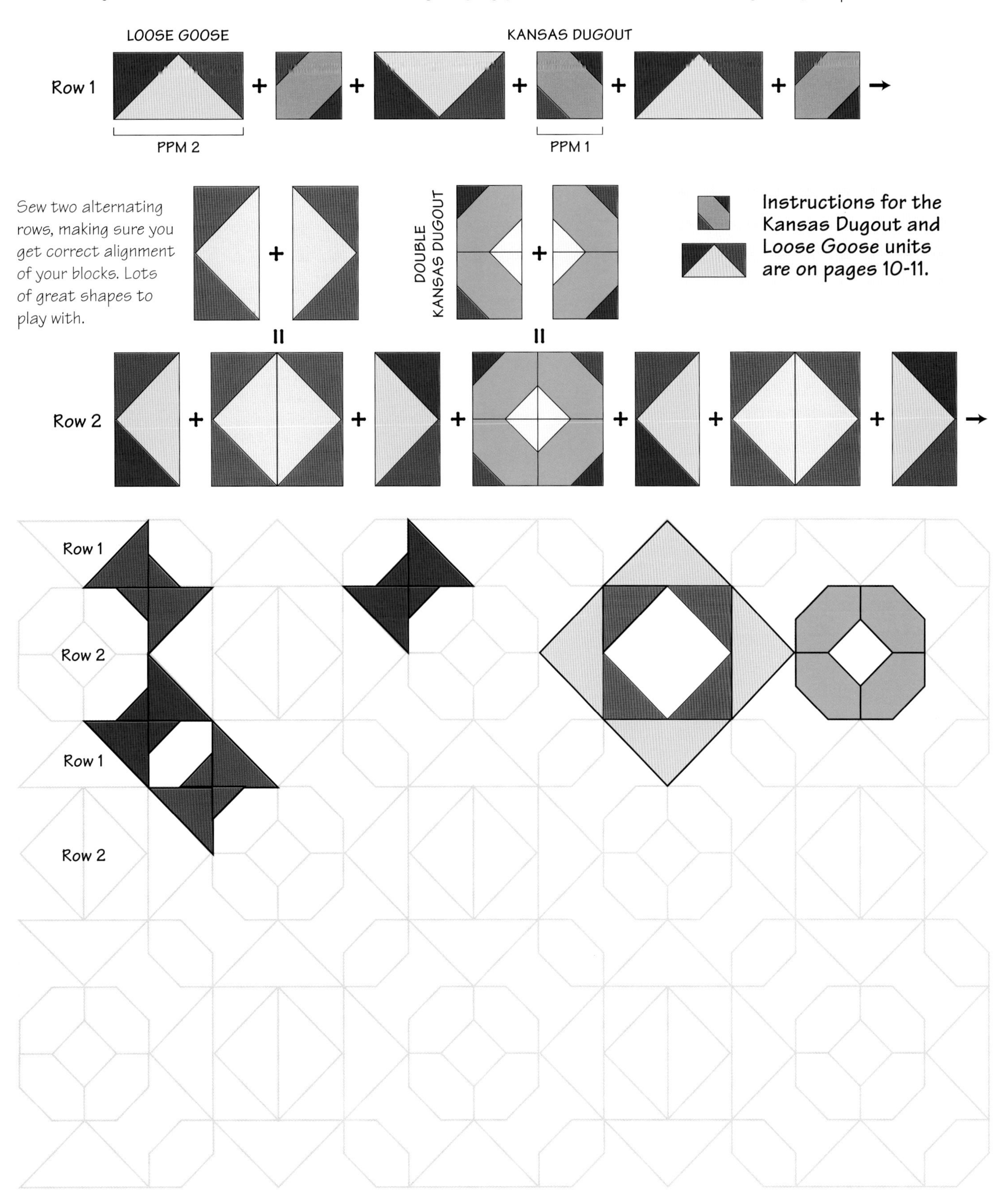

You may photocopy this page for your personal use to experiment with coloring your design; this page is not for distribution.

Pieced by Jan Krueger,
Hearthside Quilters Nook,
Hales Corner, Wis.

Pieced by Diana Marshall,
Oatley Cottage, Australia

Four Hidden Spools

Pieced by Jan Krueger,
Hearthside Quilters Nook,
Hales Corner, Wis.

Pieced by Jan Krueger,
Hearthside Quilters Nook,
Hales Corner, Wis.

Four Hidden Spools

This design is made from Double Kansas Dugout and Loose Goose units plus rectangle units that measure PPM 1 long and the width of your choice (I prefer a width that is one-half of PPM 1). The background pieces for the Kansas Dugout and Loose Goose must be your selected PPM 1 width.

You may photocopy this page for your personal use to experiment with coloring your design; this page is not for distribution.

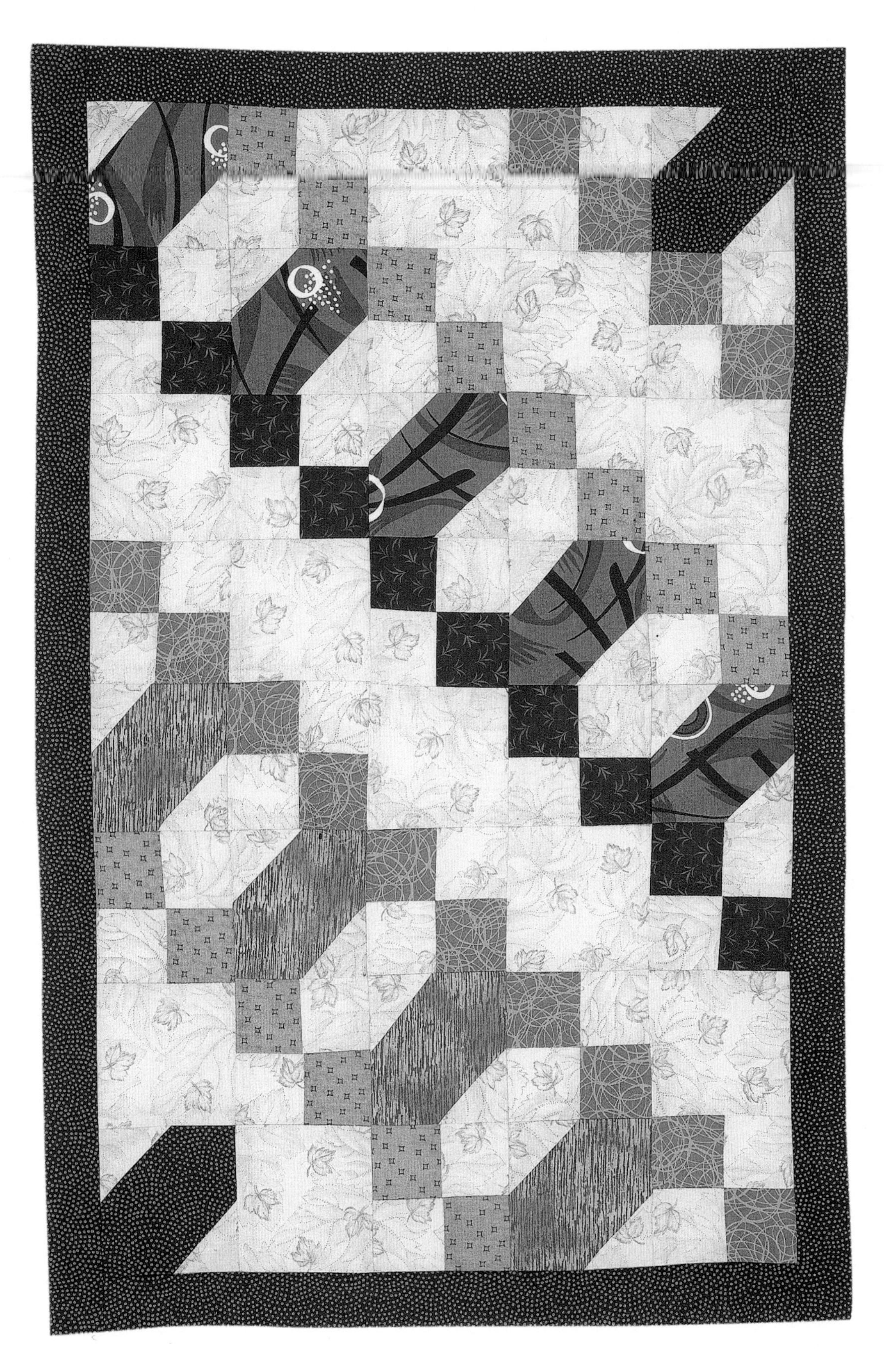

Milk Bones

Pieced by Pat Howard,
Los Angeles, Cal.

Milk Bones

This fun design can be layed out a lot of different ways; see the work pages for variations at the back of the book. Three blocks create this design: the four-patch, the Kansas Dugout, and a plain square. First make a four-patch; measure it to determine your PPM 1 for the Kansas Dugout and the plain square.

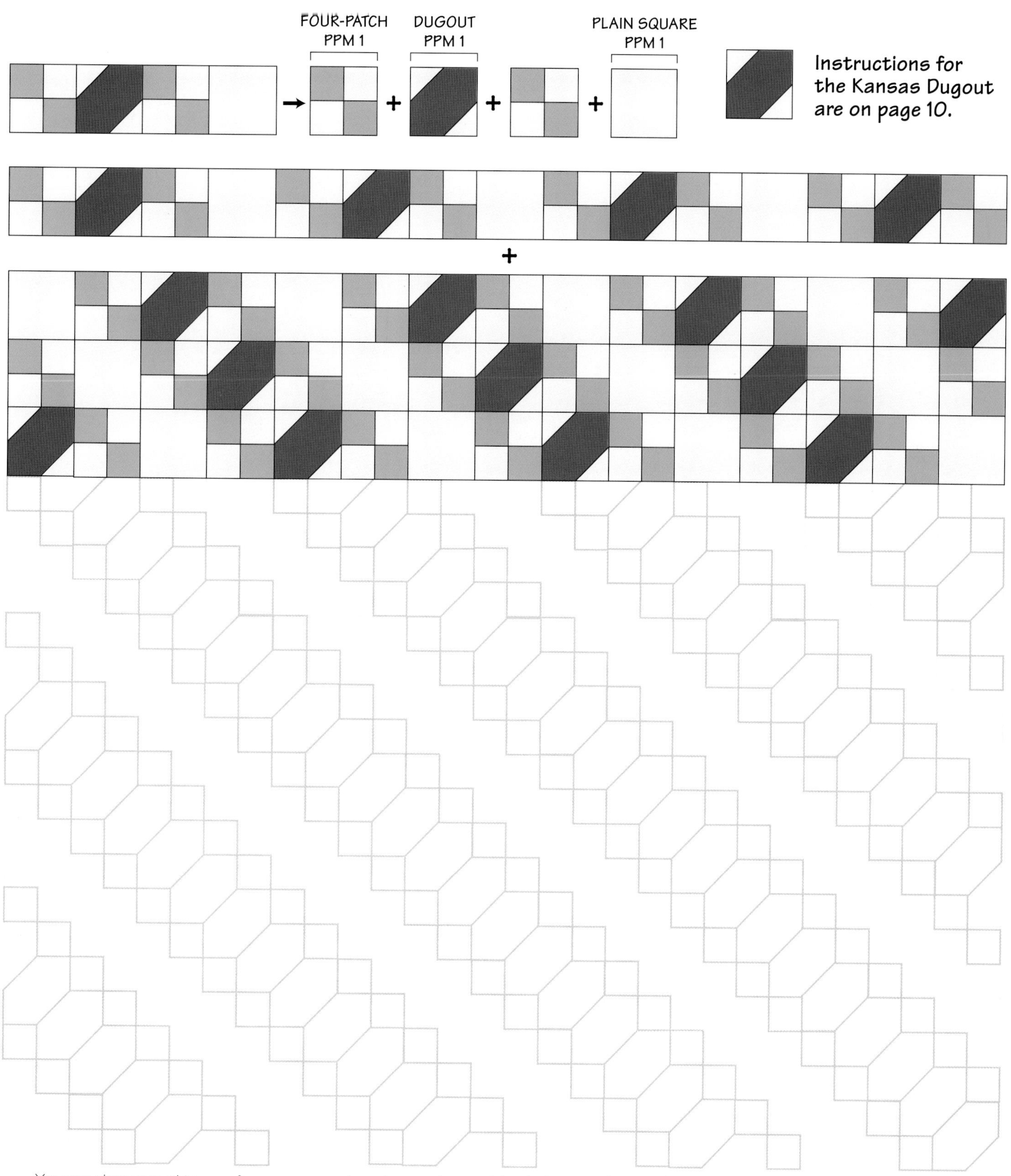

You may photocopy this page for your personal use to experiment with coloring your design; this page is not for distribution.

More Milk Bones
Variation 1 Worksheet

This design has two alternating rows.

You may photocopy this page for your personal use to experiment with coloring your design; this page is not for distribution.

More Milk Bones
Variation 2 Worksheet

Lots of great diagonal patterning to play with.

You may photocopy this page for your personal use to experiment with coloring your design; this page is not for distribution.

Lattice with a Twist

Pieced by Anne Gallo,
Yankee Quilts,
Chelmsford, Mass.

Lattice with a Twist

I really like the clean look of this design built with Double Kansas Dugouts and rectangles. You could use a different background for each large rectangle, or take the easy way out, and do a muckled-up background.

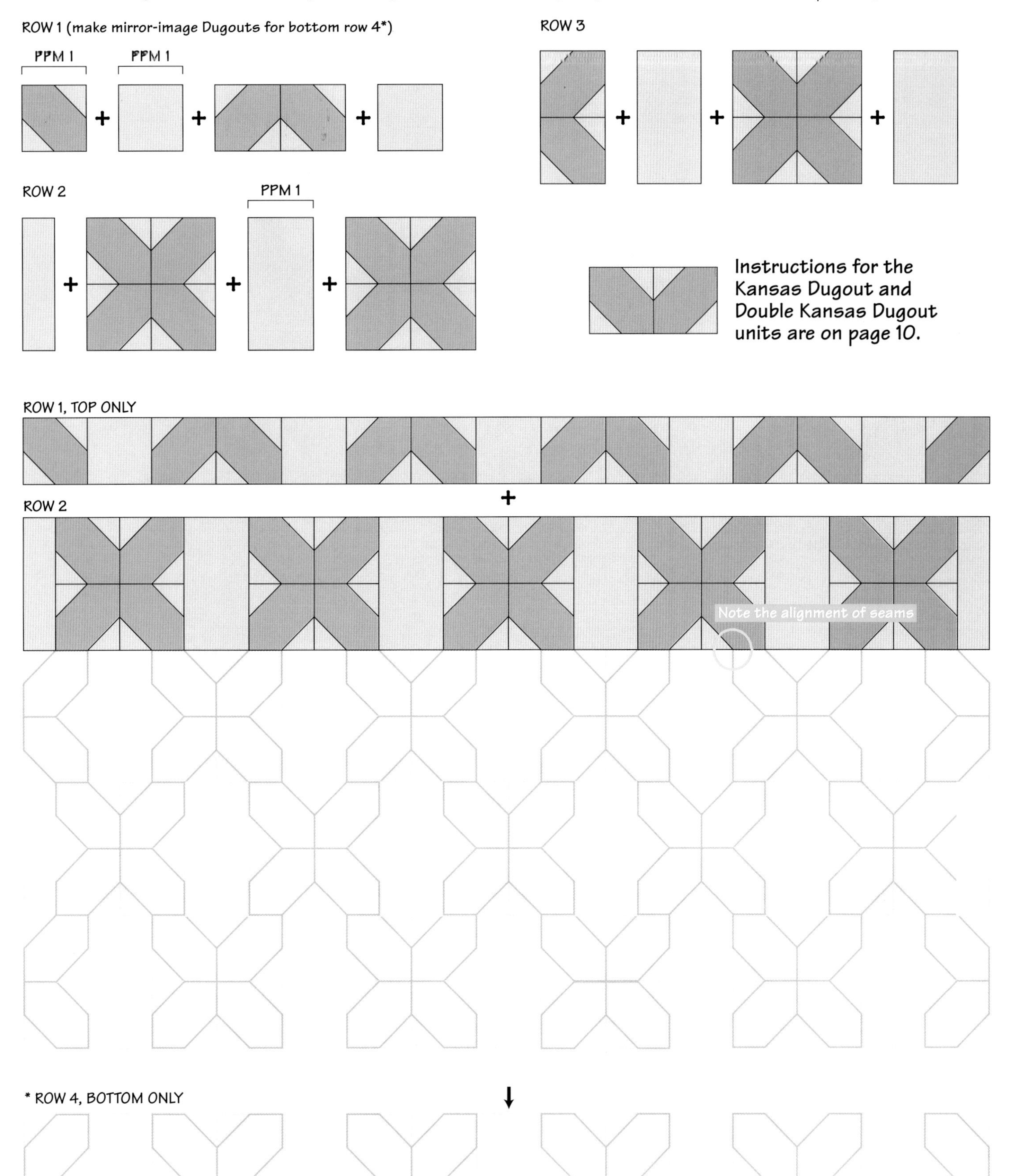

You may photocopy this page for your personal use to experiment with coloring your design; this page is not for distribution.

Pieced by Anja Hantelmann,
Rastede, Germany

Advanced Medallion

Pieced by Mary Ellen Hopkins
Pacific Palisades, Cal.

Advanced Medallion

The offset Kansas Dugouts in this pattern are not for the faint-hearted. You frequently have to "share" sections. Study the medallion pattern units and the diagram, especially noting where rectangles are used in the place of squares. This design is well worth the extra effort. Check out the quilt made by Anja Hantelmann (page 36). Not only is it terrific; she's created the "cabana" look! This quilt goes perfectly with the "at the seaside" fabric...she's good.

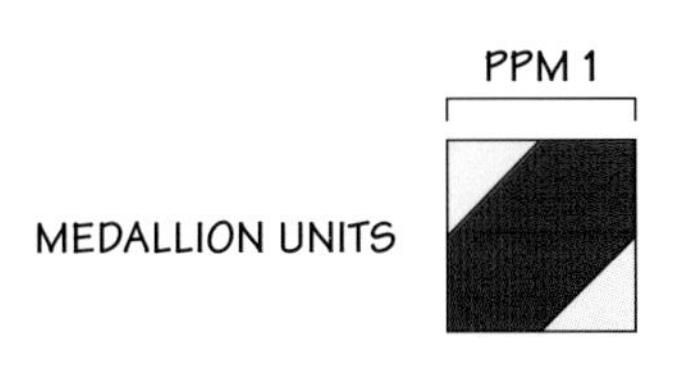

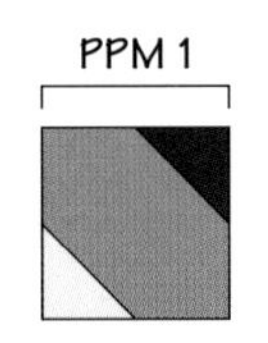

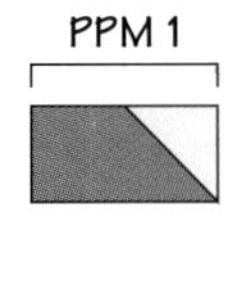

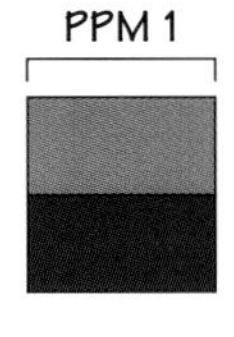

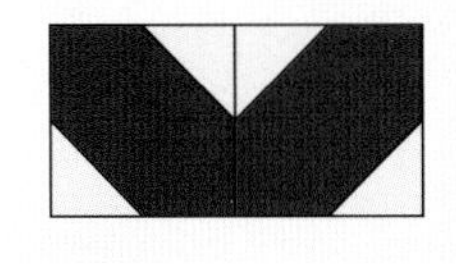

Instructions for the Kansas Dugout and Double Kansas Dugout units are on page 10.

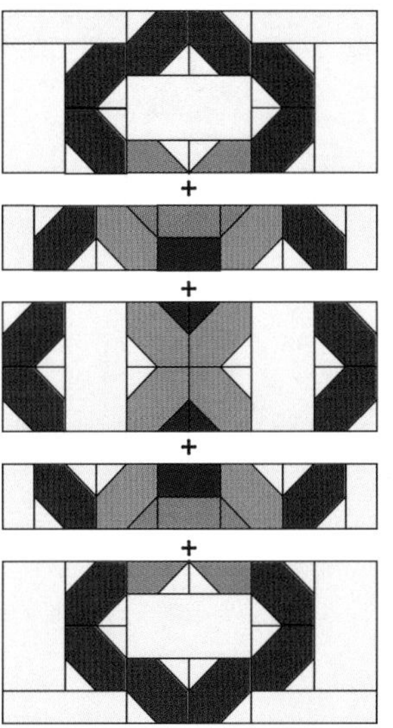

You may photocopy this page for your personal use to experiment with coloring your design; this page is not for distribution.

Loose Goose Pinwheels

Pieced by Margaret Prina,
Albuquerque, N.M.

**Pieced by Mary Beth Wiggins,
Oklahoma City, Ok.**

Loose Goose Pinwheels

This design is based on two sizes of modified Loose Goose blocks, plain squares and four-patches can be integrated for striking effects. Until you are comfortable selecting your own sizes for blocks, you may want to use the sizes shown in the illustrations.

If you are including four-patches, make them first to establish your PPM 1.

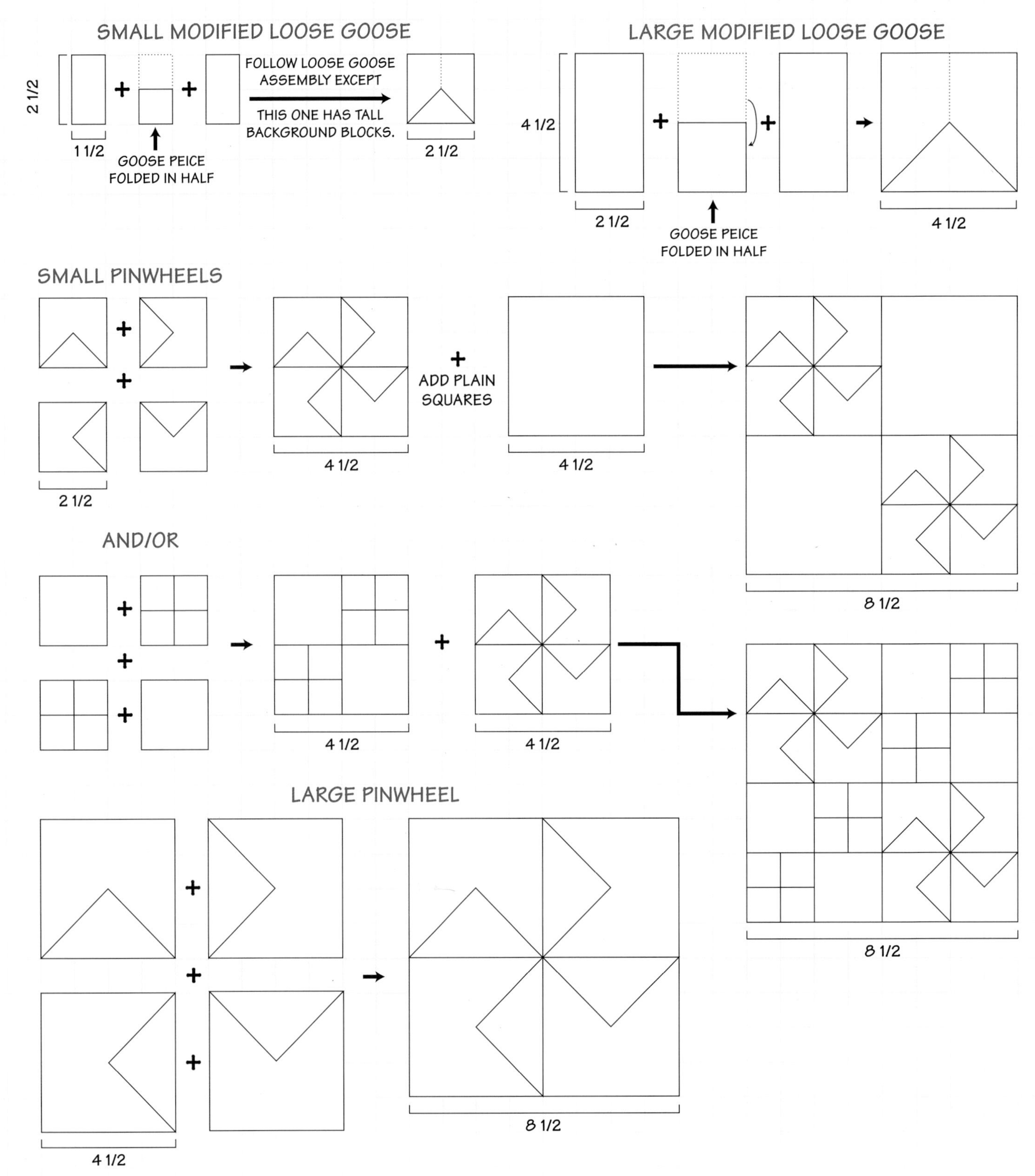

You may photocopy this page for your personal use to experiment with coloring your design; this page is not for distribution.

Loose Goose Pinwheels

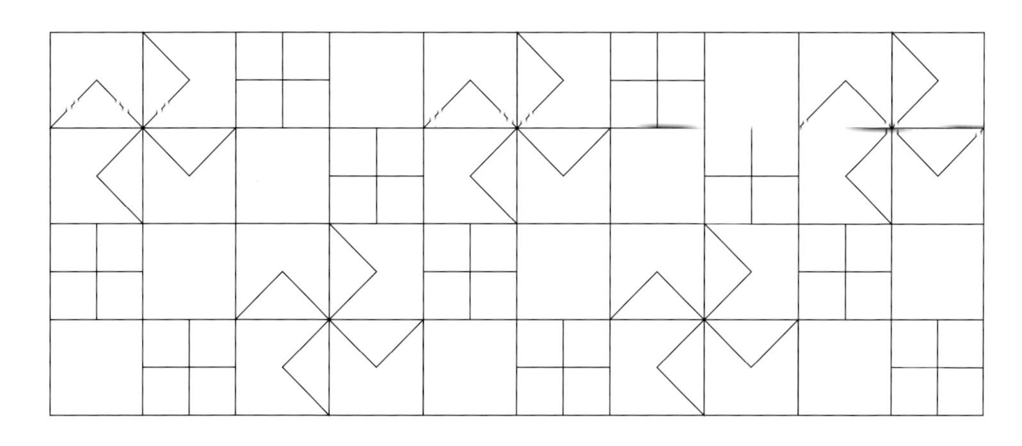

THE BLOCKS

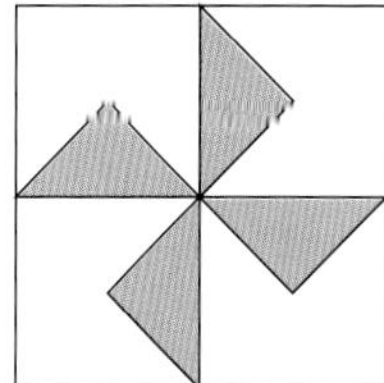

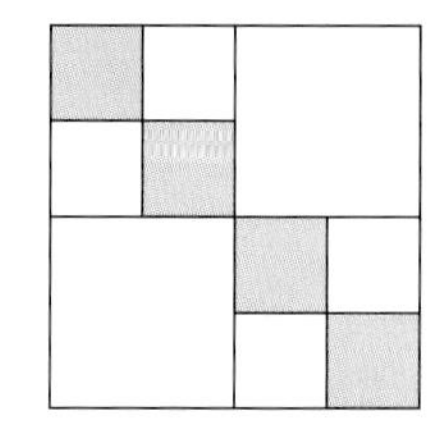

IF YOU DON'T PUT THE PINWHEELS RIGHT NEXT TO EACH OTHER YOU WON'T HAVE SUCH A "WAD" IN THE CORNERS.

SHOULD BE SCRAPS, EVEN IF YOU ONLY USE TWO COLORS, LIKE BLUES AND YELLOWS.

You may photocopy this page for your personal use to experiment with coloring your design; this page is not for distribution.

Simple Shapes

Pieced by Margaret Prina,
Albuquerque, N.M.

Simple Shapes

This is a more advanced design than most of the others in this book because you need to make eight different blocks, and you have to know how to add window paning (sashing), denoted by arrows.

This is an example block. Refer to the Kansas Dugout instructions on page 10. Note that the block in this example uses four connector squares in two different sizes. Follow the diagram to make blocks A-K in the indicated quantities.

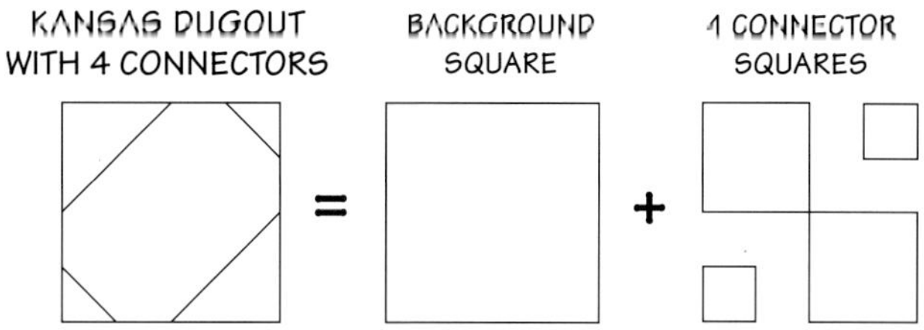

KANSAS DUGOUT WITH 4 CONNECTORS = BACKGROUND SQUARE + 4 CONNECTOR SQUARES

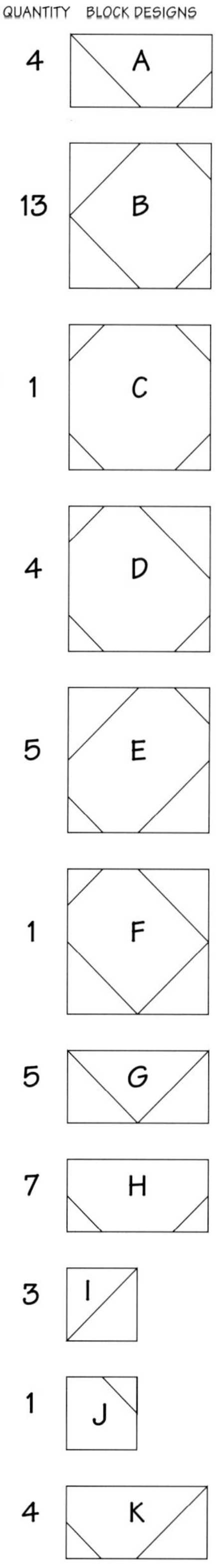

QUANTITY	BLOCK DESIGNS
4	A
13	B
1	C
4	D
5	E
1	F
5	G
7	H
3	I
1	J
4	K

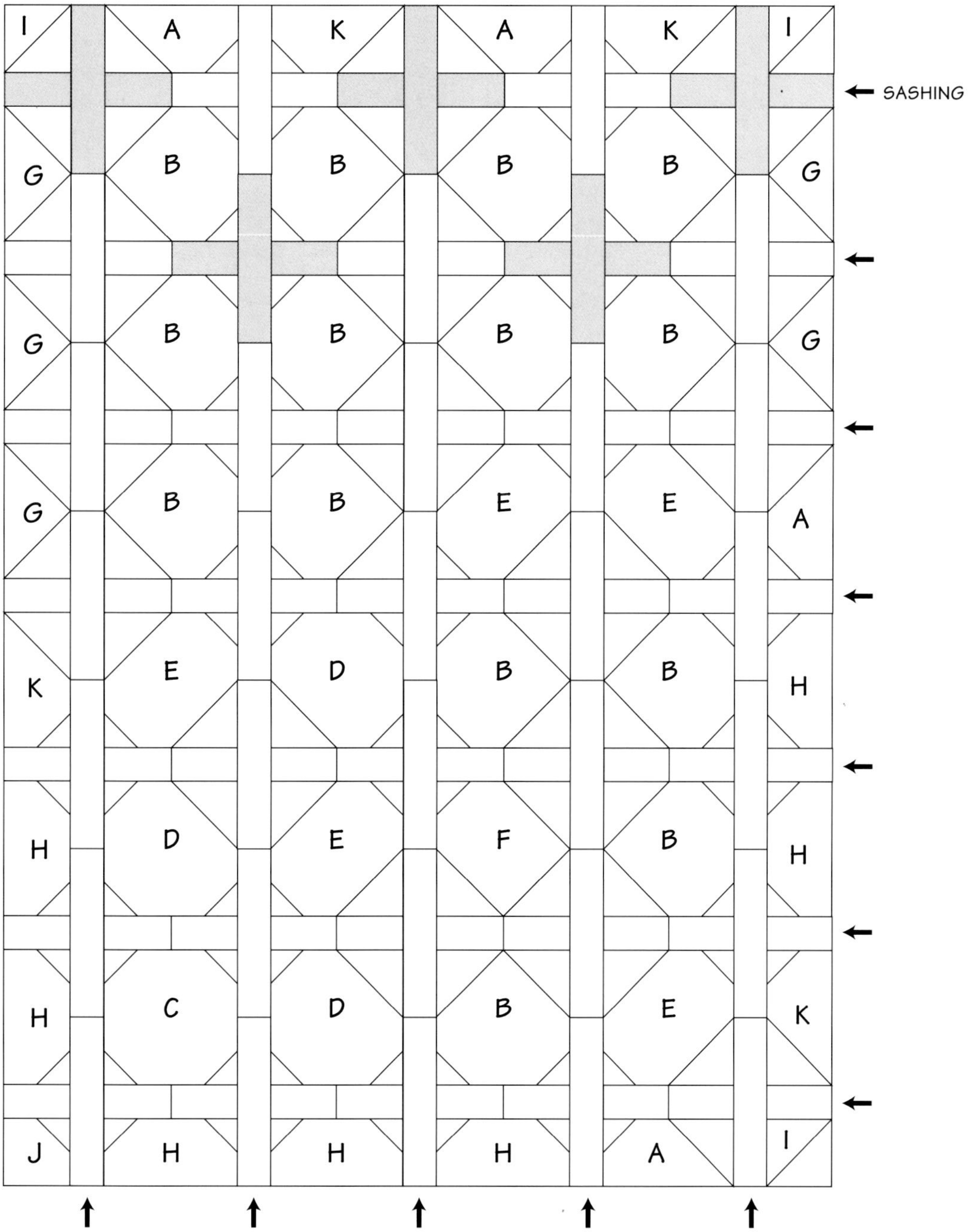

I	A	K	A	K	I
G	B	B	B	B	G
G	B	B	B	B	G
G	B	B	E	E	A
K	E	D	B	B	H
H	D	E	F	B	H
H	C	D	B	E	K
J	H	H	H	A	I

SASHING

You may photocopy this page for your personal use to experiment with coloring your design; this page is not for distribution.

Pieced by Anne Gallo,
Yankee Quilts,
Chelmsford, Mass.

Trees, Trees

Pieced by Mary Ellen Hopkins
Pacific Palisades, Cal.

Trees, Trees

Loose Goose and Kansas Dugout—the combination of these two units creates the look of a Christmas tree lot. Vary the height of the trees, stagger the rows...and then it will look like a real forest! I hope you have lots of greens—and some teal and navy blues for a touch. Work this design in groups of three horizontal rows the entire width of the quilt. Offset tree rows, and use plain rectangles according to the diagram.

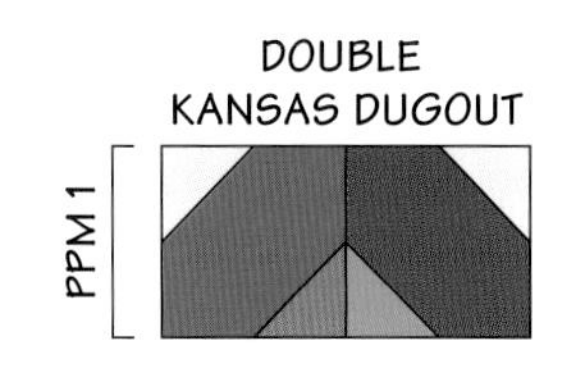

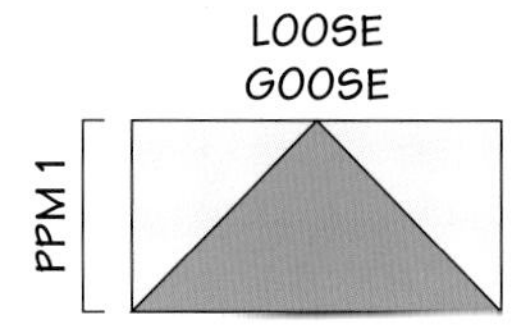

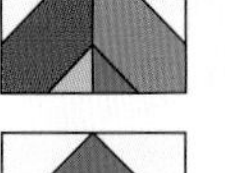

Instructions for the Kansas Dugout and Loose Goose units are on pages 10-11.

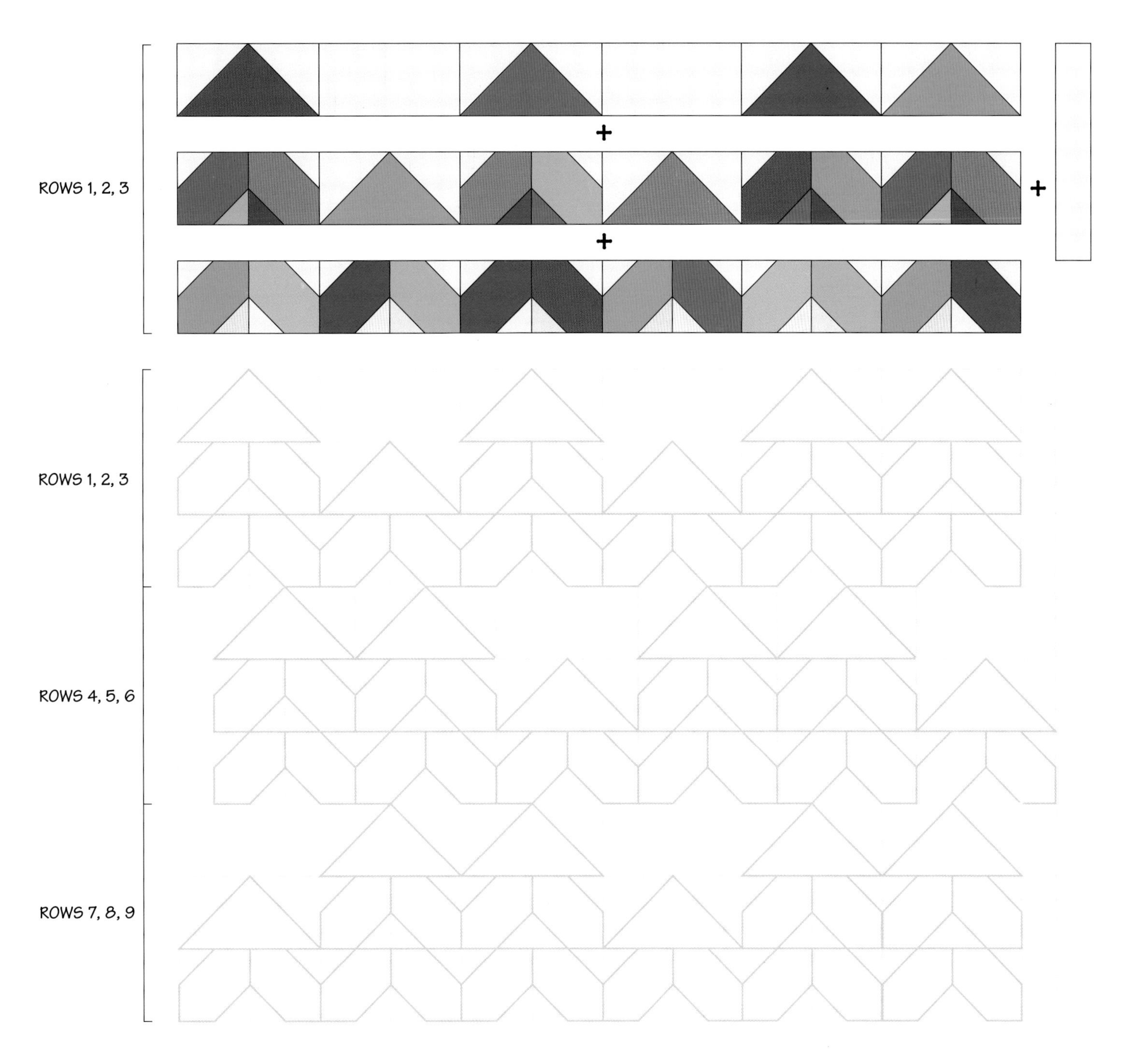

You may photocopy this page for your personal use to experiment with coloring your design; this page is not for distribution.

Scrap Loose Goose

Only one block—but, of course, **many** different fabrics. Just make a pile of Loose Goose units of mixed fabrics, get out your felt-covered work board, and go crazy.

You may photocopy this page for your personal use to experiment with coloring your design; this page is not for distribution.

Worksheet

Loose Goose Cubed

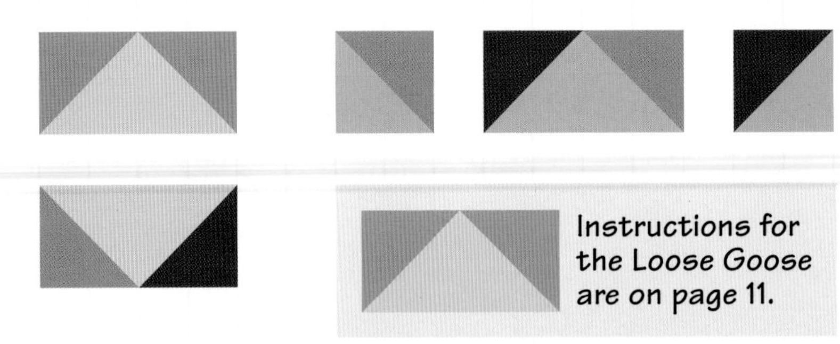

Graphically designed and pieced by JoAnn Armke

Worksheet

It Was a Very Long Flight

Designed on Lufthansa Flight #451, LAX-Frankfurt-Bremen, October 8, 1997.

A designer page. And, as you probably guessed, made from our two units, Kansas Dugout and Loose Goose. See Katrin Lehmann's quilt on page 22.

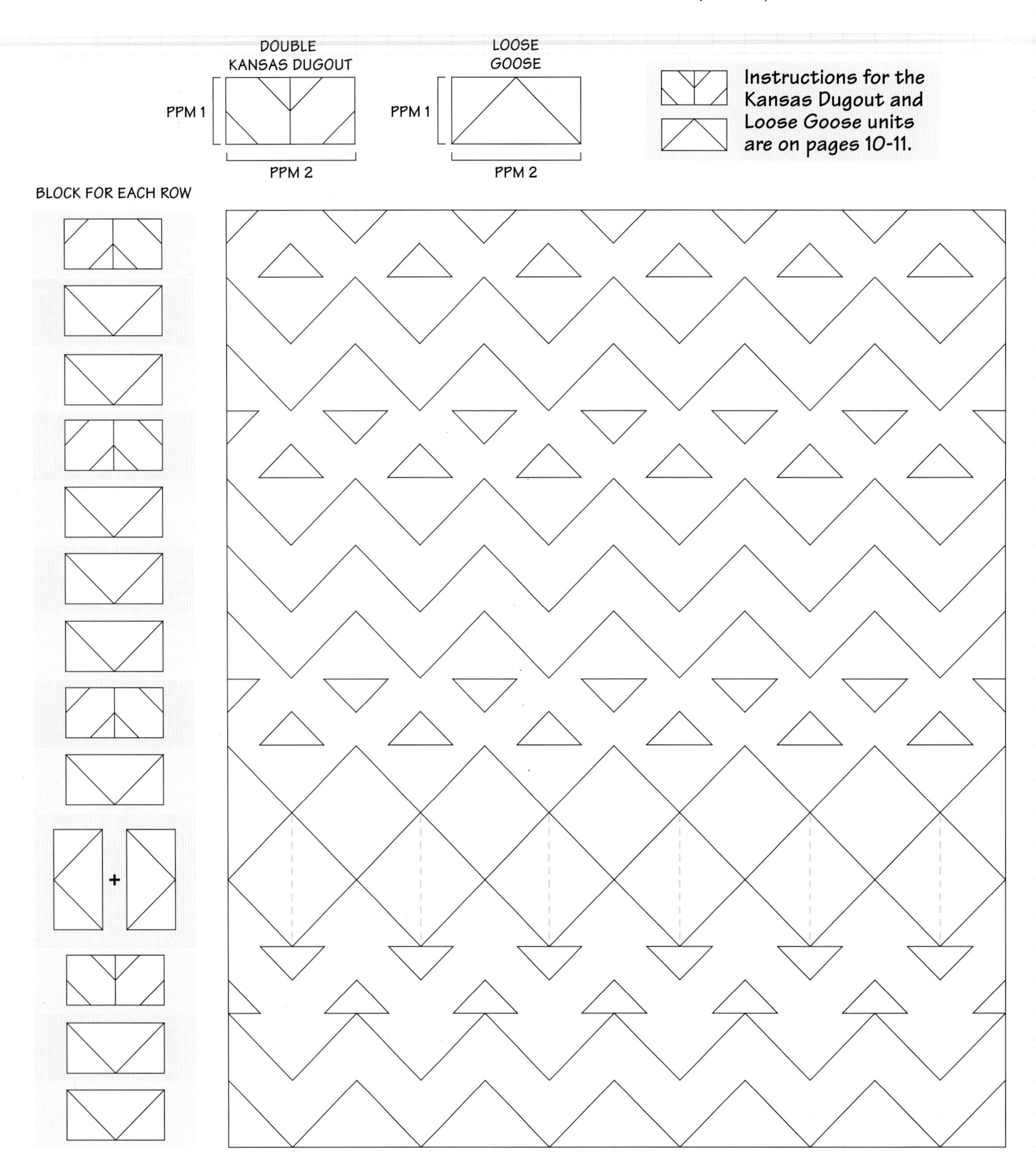

You may photocopy this page for your personal use to experiment with coloring your design; this page is not for distribution.

Worksheet

Just Messing Around

I just couldn't resist including these incomplete projects
that represent what this book is really about—**experimentation**.

This may never get finished,
but it sure was fun while it lasted.

These stars are from the Mississippi
quilt in the Kansas Connections book.

Worksheet

Oh! Those Little Kansas Dugouts!

No, there's no quilt; this is for you to play with—just rows and rows of Kansas Dugout ideas.

You may photocopy this page for your personal use to experiment with coloring your design; this page is not for distribution.

Worksheet

Worksheet

Worksheet

Mary Ellen Hopkins

She was born a long time ago in Peoria, Illinois as Mary Ellen Ingle. She lived in a lot of different cities and went to a lot of schools. She would love to hear from anyone who went to Longfellow Elementary in Detroit MI, or #44, 43 and 66 in Indianapolis, IN. Also, Shortridge High, Indianapolis, IN and Paseo High, K.C., MO. Also Drury College or Missouri University. She married a guy named Bill Hopkins, and they had four incredible children: David, Matthew, John and Barbara. She and the children lived in Santa Monica, CA from 1963 on.

She made men's shirts at home for seven years (following a stint making those awful crocheted vests). As luck would have it, she opened and ran a quilt shop, Crazy Ladies and Friends, for almost 20 years. It was a blooming success, due mainly to her clever staff. She found that getting up on a stage and being able to talk uninterrupted was a whole lot of fun. So she sold the shop and hit the road as often as possible.

Those four children married terrific people and produced seven WONDERFUL KIDS: Lindsey, Kathryn, William, Jennifer, Sara, Thomas, and Owen. Talk about a very happy lady....

What She Does...

Mary Ellen Hopkins hosts around the country a series unique programs—quilting seminars for teachers and shop owners and neighborhood shop seminars for consumers. These are three- to five-day, hands-on programs that teach methods from her book "It's Okay If You Sit On My Quilt." To get information on booking Mary Ellen for one of her programs or to see her speaking and seminar schedule visit her website, www.maryellenhopkins.com or call 800-527-2555.

Mary Ellen's publisher

ME Publications is a company created to publish Mary Ellen's books and patterns as well as those of other quilting authors. As of November 2000, Mary Ellen has published these books:

The It's Okay If You Sit On My Quilt Book

Bakers Dozen Doubled

Hidden Wells

A Log Cabin Notebook

Connecting Up

...Continuing On

Even More Well Connected

Kansas Connections

Over Under Double Disconnected
Woven Squares with Shading

The Double Wedding Ring Book

Connectors Collection

Ordering books and patterns

If you are looking for any of Mary Ellen's books and patterns, check with your local quilt shop, where you will find that many of them also teach Mary Ellen's "It's Okay" quilting methods.

To mail order books and patterns, call 800-527-2665.

Mary Ellen also has a unique website:
www.maryellenhopkins.com
where you can order her books and downloadable patterns, get details on booking her for talks or seminars and view her schedule to see when she will be appearing in your area.

Mary Ellen, global speaker

Finally, Mary Ellen speaks to quilt guilds and consumer groups around the world. She has lectured extensively in the United States, Europe, Canada, Australia and, not so extensively, in Japan, South Korea, Africa and the Middle East. This is one lady you don't want to miss!

What Is a Grandparent?

Contemplations from Mary Ellen Hopkins

Someone who always brings presents...
a. Some great
b. Some dumb

Someone who makes meals that are really weird.

Someone who can tell your mom or dad "what to do"
...in THAT voice.

Someone who you can tell anything to
and know they will never be shocked.

Someone who loves you "no matter what"
and who is very good at handling "trouble stuff".

Someone who is very good at keeping secrets.

Trust these people. They've been around the block several times.
They will help you out of any mess you're in.

Grandparents have different jobs than parents.
You will be very lucky in life if you can benefit from both.

I wrote this for my grandchildren April 20, 1999, the day of the Columbine High School tragedy, while in Portland, Maine giving a teacher seminar.